WORK
SHOP

WORK SHOP

The consumer-driven transformation of Commercial Real Estate

JOE BRADY

GRAMMAR
FACTORY
— EST⁰ 2013 —

Grammar Factory Publishing
MacMillan Company Limited
25 Telegram Mews, 39th Floor,
Suite 3906
Toronto, Ontario, Canada
M5V 3Z1

www.grammarfactory.com

Brady, Joe
Work Shop: The consumer-driven trans-
formation of Commercial Real Estate /
Joe Brady.

Paperback ISBN 978-1-998756-73-5
Hardcover ISBN 978-1-998756-75-9
eBook ISBN 978-1-998756-74-2

1. BUS054020 BUSINESS &
ECONOMICS / Real Estate /
Commercial. 2. BUS054000 BUSINESS
& ECONOMICS / Real Estate / General.
3. ARC010000 ARCHITECTURE /
Urban & Land Use Planning.

Production Credits
Cover design by Designerbility
Interior layout design by Setareh
Ashrafologhalai
Book production and editorial services
by Grammar Factory Publishing

**Grammar Factory's Carbon
Neutral Publishing Commitment**
Grammar Factory Publishing is proud to
be neutralizing the carbon footprint of
all printed copies of its authors' books
printed by or ordered directly through
Grammar Factory or its affiliated companies through the purchase of Gold
Standard-Certified International Offsets.

Disclaimer
The material in this publication is of
the nature of general comment only
and does not represent professional
advice. It is not intended to provide
specific guidance for particular circumstances, and it should not be relied on
as the basis for any decision to take
action or not take action on any matter
which it covers. Readers should obtain
professional advice where appropriate,
before making any such decision. To
the maximum extent permitted by law,
the author and publisher disclaim all
responsibility and liability to any person,
arising directly or indirectly from any
person taking or not taking action based
on the information in this publication.

CONTENTS

INTRODUCTION
CONTAINERS
OF THE PAST

THE OFFICE real estate asset class is experiencing the same market dynamics as the retail asset class did starting some twenty-five years ago. And the common denominators are technology and consumer behavior. Rapid technological advancements and evolving consumer behaviors are radically reshaping the economy, workforce, and how we live, work, and play.

Traditional commercial real estate (CRE) models that relied on long-term leases and predictable demand are grappling to adapt to this new dynamic environment. No sector has been spared from disruption, from retail stores to offices to entire downtown cores. As work becomes untethered from physical spaces and online shopping continues to augment brick and mortar, the assets that once formed the backbone of cities now risk obsolescence.

Unless commercial real estate evolves to meet modern needs, it faces becoming increasingly irrelevant. Real estate that is not deeply integrated with digital technologies, flexible to changing uses, and prioritizing the employee and customer experience will struggle to attract tenants and investors.

The next decade will separate the innovators from the laggards as the industry is forced to reckon with its lack of agility in an era of exponentially accelerating change. As writer and business leader Rishad Tobaccowala says, "The future does not fit in the containers of the past." We saw this play out in the retail industry and retail real estate. In many respects, office real estate is having a retail moment.

E-commerce retail and hybrid work are two sides of the same consumer coin. Failure to understand the implications of consumer primacy will have disastrous effects for companies, real estate owners, service providers, and the communities in which they all operate. The retail industry learned this the hard way and has taken over a decade to recover.

Consumer primacy puts consumers' needs and experiences at the forefront of planning, design, and operations. Key aspects of consumer primacy include: convenience, customer experience, flexibility, technology enablement, personalization, and engagement. Consumer primacy is enabled and propelled by technology, which leads to a duality of action. For retail, it means shopping in-store and online. In a work sense, it means working from the office, home, and "third places" (think flexible office operators, Starbucks and the like).

This is a difficult pill to swallow for those who are looking for a "silver bullet" answer. All too often, the public discourse devolves into reductive thinking. There must be an answer. In many ways, one size fits… well, one size. Perhaps the key to the future of commercial real estate lies not in better solutions and answers, but in better questions and entirely new opportunities.

Retail real estate started experiencing this existential threat some twenty-five years ago. Technology evolved, consumers adopted the technology, and retailers were required to adapt or die. While technology evolved, it did so in a way that initially simply enabled existing behaviors. (An example in another industry highlights the impact of technology on consumer behavior. Newspapers and magazines rushed to turn ink into pixels, initially failing to see how the social elements of commenting, sharing and posting were far more important than paper and screens.) Retailers moved quickly to offer online, digital alternatives to support the brick and mortar, physical store. Whole store layouts were changed to support "last mile" delivery. During the pandemic, consumers could drive to the grocery store and have workers put orders in their car trunk with no human interaction. Many who failed to evolve fell victim to irrelevancy and even bankruptcy.

As a result, the consumer gained primacy. More than ever before, consumers determined which locations and retailers were relevant—and voted with their wallets. "Shop" evolved from a noun to a verb—from a place consumers went, to something they did, irrespective of location. E-commerce, or multi-channel retail, gained in prominence as technology allowed consumers to act with agency, autonomy, and optionality (more on this later). Consumers gained power and freedom with regard to their choices.

Today, in the post-pandemic era, we are seeing the same threat thrust upon office real estate. Company employees are the new consumers. "Work," like "shop," has migrated from noun to verb—from a place we went, to a thing we do, irrespective of location. "Work" and "office" are decoupled. The pandemic created a tectonic shift, whereby employees have primacy and are voting with their feet regarding when and where they work.

While employees have gained strength, companies need to adapt and evolve. In the wake of the pandemic, one of the driving forces for RTO (return to office—a coordinated plan to bring employees back into the office following extended periods of working from home) is advancement of workplace and company culture. But culture is built on trust. When managers issue RTO edicts, they erode trust.

Mandates are counterproductive. Instead, leaders need to support their employees and create environments where it's truly advantageous for those employees to be in the office. Specifically in the keyboard economy where output is created in the form of information and data products, software and application, research and development, creative products, consultancy and expert services, intellectual property, financial products and services, and networks and platforms. Leaders need to clearly articulate times when being together in one place is essential, and curate those gatherings accordingly.

Productivity has been the holy grail for employers. Unfortunately, it has remained elusive in terms of consistent measurement. Regardless, we still hear requirements for buildings and offices based on driving productivity. As I will argue in this book, we should abandon the productivity pursuit in favor of a more germane and tangible outcome: effectiveness. Effectiveness denotes impact. Effectiveness is directly tied to the overarching success of the enterprise. In contrast, productivity is an industrial era construct. While there are still industries and jobs where productivity is important, the conceptual age of work is more reliant on effectiveness and impact. We will explore this further. But first, allow me to introduce myself properly.

A seasoned professional
with a unique perspective

I have spent much of my career in commercial real estate. I've had the opportunity to lead one of the biggest retail real estate organizations in the world, Walgreens. During the pandemic, I scaled an innovative flexible office business in the Americas. I've brokered, invested in, and developed hundreds of thousands of square feet of commercial real estate. I've rolled out retail stores in Brazil, Malaysia, China, and South Korea in addition to thousands in the United States. I've advised major corporate occupiers of office space across Europe in the wake of Brexit. In short, I've been fortunate to sit at virtually every seat at the real estate table.

As I reflect on over thirty years of deal making, advising, developing, and investing, it has become clear that the world is changing faster than ever and office real estate is struggling to keep up. We are hearing and reading about the office apocalypse in the news. The same salacious headlines and gloomy predictions were made about the retail real estate industry fifteen years ago. I have seen this movie before.

I was inspired to write this book as a call to arms for the commercial real estate industry, highlighting some of the lessons it can learn from retail. The retail sector continues to adapt; the chatter about the retail apocalypse is history. Relevant retailers, whether high-end luxury brands or daily-needs grocery stores, continue to adapt and thrive. Between 2017 and 2020, we saw 162 retail bankruptcies, accounting for 13,722 store closings. At the same time, the industry added 15,430 new stores, driven heavily by dollar store openings. Between 2022 and 2023, there were only twenty bankruptcies and 1,646 store closings. And the retail industry added another 10,500 stores, showing a steady recovery.

Figure 1: Retail Openings and Closings

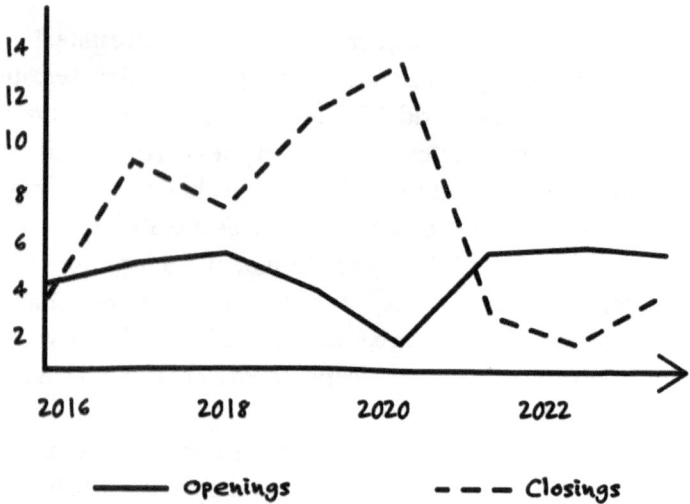

Source: PNC RE Market Research, ICSC Research

But office is a different story.

Once valued at over three trillion dollars, the office industry is grappling with apocalyptic headlines, maturing leases, and looming debt expiration. And all in the face of changing consumer/employee behavior. As we will explore, "work" and "office" are no longer intertwined—at least not to the same degree as before. The notion of working nine to five, Monday to Friday is anachronistic. We are in the conceptual age where ideas and outcomes matter.

While owners and investors of office real estate may face economic loss or even bankruptcy, the biggest issue for me is the health of communities where the real estate is located. We are seeing the beginnings of "urban doom loops" in urban cores, particularly those urban cores focused on one type of activity: work. Introduced by economist Lyman Stone in his

National Review article titled "The 'Urban Doom Loop' and the Future of American Cities", published in August 2020, an urban doom loop describes a vicious cycle of declining urban areas. It occurs when a city experiences a decrease in population (including daytime population tied to workers) and economic activity. These declines lead to reduced tax revenue, which in turn causes a decline in public services and infrastructure, further exacerbating the population and economic decline. In order to have strong cities, we will need to see investment in live/work/play oriented communities.

Creating healthy ecosystems of live/work/play

Communities rely on healthy ecosystems of live/work/play, just like nature relies on healthy ecosystems. Monocultures in nature, agricultural practices of growing the same crop over a large area every year, are vulnerable to pests and diseases, reduced biodiversity, soil degradation, and reduced resiliency.

Monocultures in real estate (workplaces focused solely on work, with little room for anything else) lead to increased vulnerability and economic risk, and reduced resilience against external changes. We are seeing the consequences of this in the Central Business Districts (CBDs) of cities like Chicago, San Francisco, Seattle, Boston, St Louis, and Philadelphia. Post-pandemic, fewer office workers mean supporting businesses languish and close. Cities lose tax revenue. City officials grapple with cutting city services or raising taxes on the remaining businesses. Neither choice is good and cities enter an urban doom loop.

Instead, communities need to focus on BBDs (better business districts). BBDs represent healthy ecosystems where people live, work, and play on a seven-day basis. The smartest and most creative people are attracted to these environments. BBDs are more resilient than traditional CBDs.

That's just one of my passion points. As a lifelong learner, I had a yearning to study the past in order to prepare for the future. I recently completed a course through Massachusetts Institute of Technology called "AI and Business Strategy" and another course, through the University of Chicago Booth School of Business, on behavioral economics. Those two classes helped solidify my thinking around accelerating technology (AI) and changing consumer behavior (behavioral economics).

In this book, I will share my thoughts and experiences around the future of commercial real estate for owners, occupiers, and communities. I will explore the history of technology and work, which go hand in hand. I will question why we still focus on agricultural and industrial era constructs. And I will explore the many lessons of relevancy (and irrelevancy) from retail, and thoughts on how the office asset class can adapt and evolve.

This book will examine technological platform shifts, the impact on retail over the last twenty years, the growing impact on work, how "old" approaches to work impact the health and wellness of workers and entire communities, the future of work (FoW), the new role of leadership, along with design, sustainability and predictive analytics. Finally, the book will conclude with predictions on the future of commercial real estate.

The three key components for consideration are:

1 Accelerating technology;
2 Changing consumer behavior; and
3 The ultimate impact on the built environment.

This book is intended for leaders who make decisions involving the built environment. Whether you are an owner, occupier, service provider, elected official or community member, the health of your community is being driven by consumers. Consumers represent seventy per cent of US GDP.

Figure 2: Three Key Components for Considerations

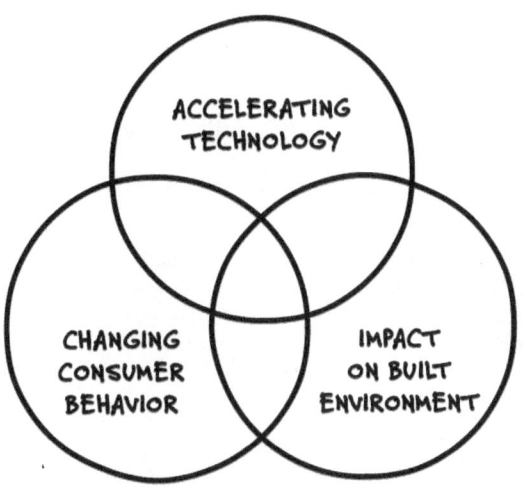

Real estate needs to become more dynamic and agile as the needs of consumers change. The retail sector was the first to experience this consumer shift. The office sector is now facing its own series of challenges, including expiring debt on properties, erosion in value, and uncertainty with renewals (research shows fifty per cent of all office leases will expire by the end of 2025).

Corporate leaders need to understand that "work" and "office" are decoupled, as I stated earlier. Many argue that employees have the upper hand given the near-full employment rate in the US economy. I submit that consumer primacy will always prevail in the keyboard economy, where effectiveness is prized over productivity. Where outcomes drive the economy. Where innovation propels whole new industries.

You will benefit from this book by having a wider picture of the changes impacting corporate real estate.

A LOOK IN THE REARVIEW MIRROR

"Software is eating the world."

MARC ANDREESSEN

THE STORY OF civilization is, in many ways, a narrative of technological innovation. Each new discovery, each push forward, has inevitably altered the way we interact with our environment and with one another. Technological platform shifts occur when there are major transitions in core technologies and infrastructures that impact or enable significant sectors of the economy and society. Each platform shift, which we will explore in detail, impacts the built environment required to support people and businesses.

Platform shifts are usually driven by new or expanding technology that provides improvements in cost, accessibility, usability, and functionality. Incumbent platforms are often disrupted by nimble startups introducing these shifts. In this chapter, I'll offer a brief history of platform shifts, with a focus on their impact, and the subsequent challenges faced by commercial real estate. But first, let's take a quick look at work through the ages, as this provides a backdrop for the platform shifts that have occurred in the last century.

A look at work through the ages

It is important to look at history for insights into how people worked, where they lived, and how technology, or lack thereof, impacted their quality of life. With each major platform shift, we see an acceleration in productivity and quality of life driven by new and emerging technologies. Jobs were invariably replaced, with even more jobs emerging to harness the power of the emerging technologies.

Agrarian age (8000 BCE–1500s)
Agriculture demanded labor centered on small-scale, locally accessible real estate augmented with handicrafts. Work was subject to both time of day and time of the year. Family units and small communities supported bartering, leading to money-based exchanges. Work was manual with a minimal level of technology. It was truly good to be the king as the monarch claimed ownership over all the land in the kingdom. The term "landlord" emerged during the era of feudalism. The king would grant portions of his land to nobles, who were his "lords." The lords generally rented the land to tenant farmers, who worked the land in exchange for rent, typically in the form of crops and commodities.

First industrial revolution (mid-1700s–late 1800s)
The first industrial revolution saw a shift from field to factory. Work became centered in factories where assembly lines, new machine tools, and emerging labor specialization emerged. Field to factory also fueled urbanization. By the end of the 1800s, over fifty per cent of the US population lived

in urban areas for the first time. Long hours, low wages, and poor conditions were common for the early industrial workers. Inventions like the telegraph, telephone, light bulb, and internal combustion engine led to the second industrial revolution. Meanwhile, agriculture became more commercial and productive, requiring fewer people to produce the same outputs. The transportation revolution occurred, with new railroads allowing bulk goods and people to move farther and faster than ever before.

Second industrial revolution (late 1800s–early 1900s)

The second industrial revolution saw revolutionary innovations that consolidated industrial supremacy through new electricity-driven and oil-fueled technologies for transportation, mass production, communication, and consumer markets. Factory mechanization reduced the need for some jobs, increased overall productivity, and created new job categories, including the role of management. Greater urbanization, increased leisure time, and different consumer lifestyles developed alongside mass production.

Cities grew horizontally and vertically, thanks in part to technological advancements in the use of steel and the electricity. The Home Insurance Building in Chicago, completed in 1885, was considered the first true skyscraper. While work was still happening in factories, office buildings emerged to meet the needs of new consumer industries and mass-produced goods targeting the growing middle class. In 1900, agriculture accounted for twenty-five per cent of GDP and forty per cent of the US workforce. By comparison, only around two per cent of the US labor force worked in farming in 2000.

Post-industrial age (1950s–1990s)

The post-World War Two era saw an acceleration in infrastructure, computers evolving from room-sized mainframes to personal computers, and transportation moving not only people and goods but information via the internet. Suburbanization grew as roadways and cars allowed workers to live in growing ring communities around urban centers. The first shopping malls emerged to quench the growing demand for consumer goods. Automation replaced some manufacturing jobs while administrative and white-collar office jobs expanded. Work still maintained elements of both agrarian and industrial era constructs with nine to five, Monday to Friday schedules, even in office settings. Advancements in communication and the internet led to increasing globalization and outsourcing of manufacturing overseas. Real estate continued to evolve and adapt, with old industrial or warehouse buildings repurposed into residential lofts and tech workplaces.

Digital age (1990s–2010s)

The digital age saw information, creativity, and services become key economic assets. Amazon was founded in 1994 and went public in 1997. Facebook was founded in 2004 and Steve Jobs unveiled the first iPhone in 2007. Cloud computing emerged to further bolster the power and accessibility of mobile apps. Young professionals returned to downtown living, revitalizing former industrial areas into mixed-use neighborhoods. While the impact of the global financial crisis cannot be understated, the speed of technology and consumer mobility helped dig the global economy out of a deep recession.

The emergence of e-commerce saw many traditional retailers fail, leading to the closure of thousands of stores. In other instances, e-commerce complemented in-store activity and vice versa. Research has shown the presence of brick-and-mortar stores actually increased online sales revenue in certain trade areas. Conversely, the closing of a store was shown to decrease online sales in that same trade area.

Conceptual age (2015–present)

The world moved from the digital age to the conceptual age in the early 2010s as ubiquitous smartphone adoption, cloud computing, high-speed internet, 5G connectivity, and big data all heralded the biggest technological leap in human history. Increasing priority was given to user experiences, conceptual and creative skills, design thinking, and customization. Routine digital tasks were increasingly automated. We saw the explosive emergence of generative AI (GenAI) in 2022, most notably in the form of platforms like ChatGPT, the impacts of which we will explore in a later chapter.

Most importantly, the world experienced a pandemic, which created a tectonic shift in how and where consumers worked. E-commerce as a percentage of total retail sales moved from eleven per cent in 2019 to 16.5 per cent at the height of the pandemic. Estimates show the percentage rising to around twenty per cent by 2027.

Figure 3: E-Commerce Retail Sales as a Percent of Total Sales

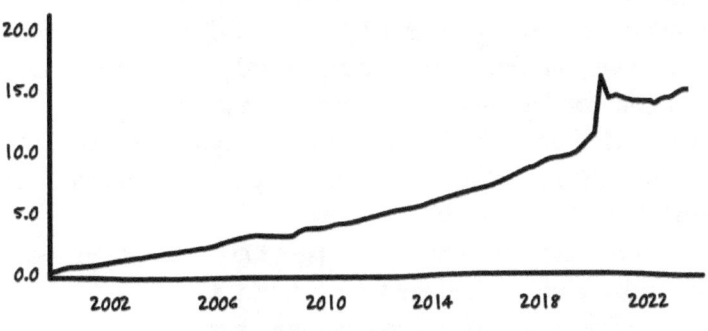

Source: U.S. Census Bureau

The pandemic forever changed consumer work behavior. After spending over two years predominantly in at-home working environments, consumers (employees) adopted more live/work activities. They had more time, and more disposable income, as a result of not physically commuting to an office. Even when the pandemic subsided, things were never the same. The average time spent in the office moved from four-plus days per week to two and a half days per week.

A brief history of platform shifts

To gain a better understanding of the impact of technology on consumer behavior, let's delve deeper into some of the most important technological milestones in recent history. This will help you appreciate the potential and power of technology over the next five to ten years. Specifically, how these exponential changes will impact consumers and the real estate in which they live, work and play.

Mainframes to personal computers

In the 1960s and 1970s, mainframe computers were the dominant computing platform for businesses and institutions. IBM set many of the standards in mainframe design and functionality. UNIVAC (Universal Automatic Computer) helped introduce mainframes into business and governmental organizations for data processing tasks. Control Data Corporation, or CDC, led by supercomputer pioneer Seymour Cray, made some of the faster supercomputers and biggest mainframes from the 1960s onward.

Mainframes were primarily used for large data processing tasks related to census taking, finance, and so on. They required very large, dedicated rooms with specialized cooling. In 1959, the IBM 7090 mainframe measured 3.6 meters by

1.5 meters by 1.7 meters (9.18 cubic meters), weighed around 9,000 pounds, had a processing speed of roughly 100 kilohertz, and had a memory of 128 to 1,024 kilobytes (water cooled). In comparison, a modern laptop measures 31.7 centimeters by 21.6 centimeters by 1.9 centimeters (1,300 cubic centimeters), weighs 3.5 pounds, has a clock speed of three gigahertz, has eight to thirty-two gigabytes of memory, and is several thousand times more powerful.

Personal computers were designed for individual/personal use rather than shared use. I remember experiencing this platform shift. As a young electrical engineering student, I felt lucky to be part of the first class at Villanova University using the new VAX-11/780 mainframe computer from Digital Equipment Corporation (DEC). We were the first class not required to use punch cards in the old IBM mainframe. Before the VAX, engineering students would need to "program" using punch cards. They had to physically input the necessary ones and zeros needed to drive programming languages like FORTRAN, COBOL, and BASIC. Users had to ensure that scores and scores of punch cards were in the right order and orientation. Many a day was ruined when gravity took hold and the punch cards were dropped and jumbled . . .

The platform shift from mainframes to PCs started the untethering process from terminal to mobile keyboard. Previously, if you wanted to accomplish any processing activity, you were bound to the location of the mainframe and adjacent terminals. Even if it was the office of the university building, users were required to ply their trade in a factory-like setting.

The PC allowed activity to happen in more diverse locations, although early connectivity and internet usage required a hard connection. From a real estate perspective, companies and institutions were able to reclaim the rooms formerly occupied by mainframes for more direct engagement and use by employees and colleagues.

Wired to wireless telephones

There was a time when you actually called someone's house. We were tied to the landline for communication and connectivity. Even the early internet days were tethered to terra firma. The cellular technology boom in the 1990s drove wireless engagement and non-stop envy. Remember those cellular antennas on cars? Some entrepreneurs made tons of cash by selling fake antennas, just so you could look cool and hip, as if you had a phone in your car.

There's no more seminal moment in untethering than Gordon Gecko, standing on a beach in the Hamptons, talking to Bud Fox, in the movie *Wall Street*. Gecko, a character made famous for his "greed is good" mantra, was talking on his Motorola brick phone (a DynaTAC 8000X), which cost 3,995 dollars in 1987 (or 11,885 dollars in today's dollars). Today, we take for granted the fact that you can call anyone, anywhere, at any time. Even apps like WhatsApp make the cost of long-distance calls essentially free.

The combination of untethering from both mainframe computers and landlines allowed consumers to gain more freedom and agency in where and how they conducted personal and professional business. The rise of the cell phone, augmented by the beauty and design of products like the iPhone, allowed people to realize their dream of talking on the beach (or anywhere they liked), like Gordon Gekko.

Physical to cloud computing

Enterprise computing shifted from on-premise servers to a cloud model starting in the 2000s. Traditionally, businesses owned and operated their own physical servers and data centers to host computing infrastructure and applications. This required large capital investment and ongoing maintenance. The real estate requirements and the need for constant "up time" resulted in significant operating expenses as well. Downtime was not an option.

With the rise of cloud computing, businesses were able to leverage servers, storage, databases, software, analytics, and more on hosted platforms by providers like Amazon Web Services (AWS), Google Cloud, Azure, and others. This provided a flexible, pay-as-you-go service. It greatly reduced the capital expenditure and operating expenditure requirements of owning and running your own data center.

One of the larger implications stemmed from obsolescence avoidance. Running a data center was like running a business. For many companies, their core business function was likely not data center management. With technology increasing and new innovations emerging at a frequency of months, not years, companies were able to take advantage of cloud providers that were constantly innovating and updating.

This meant fewer on-premise data center jobs, replaced by cloud-related roles. Those roles included cloud architects, cloud security, and cloud app developers. The platform shift from physical data centers to cloud computing allowed businesses to be more responsive, innovative, and focused on their core business goals.

The emergence of GenAI

Some call the emergence of GenAI more important than electricity and even the discovery of fire. There are multiple characteristics of the GenAI platform shift, including scale and pace, the intelligence factor, the transformation potential, and trust or ethical factors.

Compared with other platform shifts, GenAI evolved quickly from a relatively narrow research approach to a commercially viable platform, accessible by millions of consumers much faster than any other platform shifts. The low marginal cost of deploying AI models also enables remarkably wide reach.

Unlike hardware or software platforms, GenAI has some capacity to process information, to reason, and to learn and respond adaptively. This introduces an entirely different level of complexity in terms of systemic impacts compared to inert tools.

GenAI is a tool and is therefore susceptible to misuse or misinterpretation. The "black box" nature of large language models, as well as the propensity for biases and control issues, introduces completely new ethical dimensions relative to previous platforms. Maintaining responsibility and trust remains a burning topic for the leaders in GenAI as well as government regulation. The potential for misuse is extraordinary. Just like Oppenheimer questioned his groundbreaking work on the atomic bomb, the founders of OpenAI and Turing Award winner Geoffrey Hinton, the godfather of deep learning and an early pioneer in neural networks, remain outspoken about the potential existential threat associated with unchecked AI.

GenAI will invariably impact existing jobs in and around highly automatable tasks through responsibilities like data collection and processing, pattern recognition, and production and services. Here's a list of potentially impacted roles:

- **Customer service reps:** AI is automating simple queries, conversations, and sentiment analysis.

- **Food counter workers:** Self-service ordering and AI-powered kitchens can displace workers.

- **Administrative assistants:** AI is automating scheduling, documentation, and more.

- **Telemarketers:** Natural language AI can conduct sales calls and outreach.

- **Paralegals and legal assistants:** Contract review, research, and case prep automation will expand.

- **Software developers:** AI coding assistants and generative programming supplement human efforts initially.

While job displacement will invariably occur, new jobs will harness the power of GenAI. We are in the early innings of adoption and exploitation, but likely areas of new job growth include:

- **AI trainers:** Experts needed to provide domain-specific data to train AI models within sectors like healthcare, law, customer support, and so on.

- **Prompt engineers:** The key to extracting the optimal information is asking better questions. Once the large language models (LLMs) are trained, prompt engineers will develop creative queries to extract specific and precise output. There are many use cases, from medical diagnosis to critical infrastructure management to real estate portfolio management.

- **AI designers:** Hybrid user experience and machine learning experts who focus on human-centered design of AI assistants, conversational agents, and related systems.

- **AI ethicists:** Specialists who provide guidance around responsible development and deployment of AI systems so they align with ethical principles on things like fairness, accountability, and transparency.

- **AI operations engineers:** IT professionals who manage deployment, monitoring, and optimization of GenAI in production environments. Managing office and retail buildings will be augmented by GenAI, tied to IoT

(Internet of Things) sensors. No longer will buildings be down for extended periods because really smart buildings will inform managers about preventive maintenance and repairs before failures occur.

The rate of change of the rate of change

For each of the platform shifts, we see a real-world, built-environment need to adapt and evolve. Nowhere is this clearer than in the realm of real estate, where every structure we build is a reflection of our current technological capabilities and cultural norms. There are dramatic impacts on users, or, as I refer to them, consumers. Both in the retail and office setting, consumers engage in and participate in activities in the built environment.

But the rate of change OF the rate of change is accelerating. Consider the amount of time it took for different consumer products to reach 100 million users:

The telephone (1876): 51 years
Television (1926): 26 years
Mobile phones (1973): 16 years
Amazon Prime (2005): 15 years
Facebook (2003): 12 years
Pokémon Go (2016): 1 year
TikTok (2016): 9 months
ChatGPT (2022): 2 months
Threads (2023): 5 days

Venture capitalist and software engineer Marc Andreessen is famous for saying, "Software is eating the world." Maybe software was just the appetizer. It's becoming more and more evident that advanced technology, driven by GenAI and synthetic biology (more on this later), are the main course.

We are approaching the limits of Moore's law. Gordon Moore, cofounder of Intel, posited in 1965 that the number of integrated circuits on a chip would double every eighteen months, while the cost would be reduced by fifty per cent. That trend continues to hold true and, when you double power and cut costs by half for fifty years, you see an incredible exponential curve.

Figure 4: Moore's Law predicts that the transistor count on microchips doubles every two years

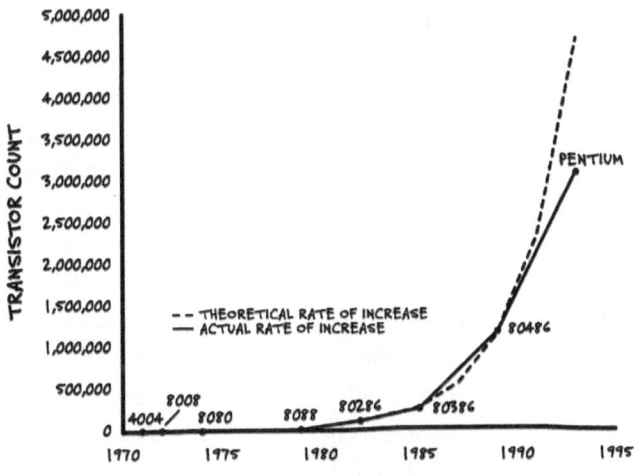

Source: Wikipedia, Moore's Law and Intel

Similarly, consider the iPhone, arguably one of the most successful and prolific products in the world. The average iPhone, with almost unlimited access to apps via the App Store, combines and replaces over fifty other tools, gadgets, and devices. The iPhone 15 has approximately 100,000 times the processing power of the computer that landed man on the Moon over fifty years ago. The exponential impact of doubling power and halving costs will continue to have bigger and more impactful benefits in our personal and professional lives.

As we've seen from Moore's law, the rate of change continues to increase, particularly when you consider Gordon Moore posited his theory in 1965. Many futurists, like Ray Kurzweil and Paul Saffo, are known to share a similar sentiment. Namely, that today is the slowest day of change for the rest of our lives. Change will continue accelerating with each platform shift.

Why is this important? Because traditional corporate real estate has historically been based on a ten-year cycle. When you compare the exponential acceleration from technology (read: Moore's law) with the traditional commercial real estate cycles, you see an incongruity. The incongruity is further exacerbated by strong inertia in the commercial real estate markets.

The inertia of the combined retail and office markets, topping seven trillion dollars, means that it's difficult to steer the ship and course correct. Inertia is the tendency of an object to resist any change in its state of motion. In science, the inertia of an object is directly proportional to its mass. More mass (read: industry size) means more resistance or inertia. Agility is the ability to move quickly and easily. While CRE is striving to talk the agility game, few are actually delivering on the mandate. Inertia is powerful.

The establishment is based on the ten-year lease agreement. Lenders want to lend at ten-year intervals. Investors depend on leveraged returns based on loans. Developers and owners are dependent upon what lenders and investors demand. Tenants are subject to the overwhelming forces above them. Consider the fact that there's a "lord" in "landlord" and "ant" in "tenant."

Compounding the challenge is the uncertainty around FoW and the future role of the office. Amid all of these changes, what is CRE to do? How can a midcap tech company, for example, sign a ten-year lease when its business model is likely stale in six months? Later, we will explore ways for CRE to synchronize with the technological age of acceleration.

Real estate has a proven ability to adapt and evolve. At the heart of our earliest advancements was the wheel. While today it seems rudimentary, its invention ushered in a new era of transportation and logistics, allowing civilizations to expand and trade over vast territories. As trade routes flourished, so did the need for infrastructure, prompting the establishment of inns, trading posts, and larger urban centers. The land around these hubs became prized real estate.

Fast forward to the Industrial Revolution, and we see the steam engine, the telegraph, and electricity playing transformative roles. Factories required workers, and workers needed homes. This led to the rapid expansion of cities and the birth of the modern suburb. Once again, real estate evolved to support the technology-driven needs of society.

Employees were required to work in the factories because that's where the machines were located. In contrast, today's digital revolution has decentralized where and how work is done. Offices are no longer the sole hubs of professional life. Homes, coffee shops, and even parks have become viable workplaces, thanks to the portability of technology.

From supercomputers to smartphones, our world is more connected, more automated, and more data-driven than ever. The real estate implications? A demand for smart homes, connected offices, and urban spaces that can seamlessly integrate with this tech-driven world.

As we journey forward in this book, it's vital to understand that technology doesn't just "happen." Every innovation is a solution to a problem, a response to a need. Real estate, from the homes we live in to the offices we work in, must evolve in tandem with these technological shifts. The very essence of "value" in property is being redefined by our technological progress.

In the chapters that follow, we will delve deeper into the many ways accelerating technology impacts our lives and reshapes the landscapes, both literal and metaphorical, of our world.

CHAPTER SUMMARY

Technological innovations have long driven and enabled transformations in how humans interact and organize themselves across societies. Major platform shifts occur when emerging infrastructures significantly impact economic and social systems. Key examples explored include the transition from mainframe computers to personal computing, landline phones to wireless mobiles, on-premise enterprise computing to cloud-based services, and now artificial intelligence.

Each shift enabled greater capabilities and efficiencies. At the same time, these disruptions required adaptations by users as well as physical spaces like real estate. Work patterns and locations changed as technology untethered processes from previous constraints like centralized factories. The rate of change has dramatically accelerated in recent decades as per Moore's law, but real estate planning cycles remain lengthy.

AI represents an exceptionally consequential shift given the scale and speed of diffusion so far. It also demonstrates more technological intelligence and autonomy than prior innovations. While promising immense productivity potential, AI threatens to automate many existing jobs. However, it will also generate new labor needs and categories. Managing such workforce transitions remains critical.

Historically, technological progress shaped settlements and infrastructure to support societal needs in areas like trade, manufacturing, and knowledge-intensive industries. Today's digital and AI revolution carries possibly more far-reaching implications across economic, governmental, and urban domains. The businesses and regions that can artfully adapt to enable human-machine synergy will likely thrive most.

Corporate real estate is one sector grappling with these platform shifts in profound ways. Location constraints around work are dissolving as cloud computing and remote collaboration tools proliferate. Yet the purpose and layout of offices is contested given the (still important) need for in-person community. Balancing flexibility with predictability across distributed workforces raises structural questions and cultural challenges.

2

THE NEW-COLLAR ECONOMY

*"Every new beginning comes
from some other beginning's end."*

SENECA

THE MARCH OF progress has always gone hand in hand with anxieties about the future. As technology integrates deeper into our lives, one of the most pervasive fears is that of job displacement. This fear isn't unfounded, nor is it new. Throughout history, every significant technological leap has faced resistance, often rooted in the apprehension of job loss. The speed of replacement, retraining, and new jobs has a dramatic impact on the built environment. Do we need the same space as we did five years ago? Is the design conducive to new and adapted work in the future?

The technology boogeyman is not something new. You only need to look at the most well-known economic theory from twentieth century economist Joseph Schumpeter. "Creative destruction" refers to the process in capitalism whereby new innovations and technologies continually disrupt and replace older ones. Schumpeter saw this constant change and dynamism as an essential driver of economic growth. He also emphasized entrepreneurship as the major catalyst propelling change and sustaining long-term economic growth. He viewed entrepreneurs as disrupters who transform markets with new products, processes, and business models.

Applying Schumpeter's theory to the GenAI era, we see a reduction in business cycles. Clusters of major innovations and technological change introduced by entrepreneurs are happening faster and faster. This acceleration is yet another reason to evolve your thinking around the built environment. Where and, more importantly, how people work in the conceptual age remains the key question for business leaders and property owners alike.

I find it important to provide historical context behind ideas and concepts provided. All too often, we look at the latest content on social media and use that to shape our worldview. So, let's take a look at jobs and work over time. From there, we'll explore the modern workplace landscape, including "new-collar" jobs, the impact on the built environment, and the future role of CRE.

A look back: jobs lost and jobs gained

The Luddite movement of the early nineteenth century is perhaps one of the most iconic representations of job replacement fear. As mechanized looms were introduced in the textile industry, skilled artisans, fearing unemployment, took to destroying these machines. They saw them as threats to their livelihoods. However, while the immediate consequence was a reduction in some specialized roles, the Industrial Revolution brought about an explosion of new jobs in factories, logistics, and even in machine maintenance.

In the twentieth century, the advent of the automobile led to a decline in professions related to horse-driven transportation. In New York City in 1900, over 30,000 people were employed to clean up the 1.5 million pounds of horse manure left on the streets each day. The 100,000 horses in the city produced over 60,000 gallons of urine daily. The sanitation and pollution issues associated with horsepower drove innovation around cleaner and safer forms of transportation, like electric street cars and the automobile. As a result, blacksmiths, carriage makers, and stable jobs dwindled. But in their place arose a plethora of opportunities in car manufacturing, mechanics, road construction, and infrastructure development.

At their height in the 1940s and 1950s, there were over 450,000 switchboard operators in the United States. Today, there are very few human switchboard operators. The 1960s saw the introduction of automated telephone switching systems. Instead of the manual pushing and pulling of jacks to initiate or terminate calls, the industry gave way to more sophisticated and higher paying jobs like network engineering technicians, computer programmers, network designers and architects, call center and customer service representatives, and voice or data network administrators. So, while almost half a million jobs were wiped out by technology, estimates show there are over one million higher skilled, higher paying jobs supporting the global digital infrastructure today.

Around 1950, at the height of gas station development, gas station attendants accounted for 500,000 to 600,000 jobs in the US. Today, with mandates from multiple US states, there are only 8,000 service station attendants, according to the U.S. Bureau of Labor Statistics. That's an extraordinary reduction of ninety-eight per cent, driven by technology and automation. Aside from New Jersey and Oregon, all other states have transitioned to self-serve setups. Gas station attendants have moved on to other jobs. Requirements to upskill and reskill were required to continue in the automotive business in jobs related to mechanics, service, and sales.

The narrative is clear: with every technological shift, certain jobs fade away, but new ones emerge. And the new jobs often outnumber the old ones, leading to an economic push.

The modern workplace landscape

Here are some of the defining traits of the modern workplace landscape...

Automation and AI

Today's landscape is dominated by discussions around AI, automation, and robotics. The concerns are valid. Automated checkouts, AI-driven customer service, and robotics in manufacturing are slowly replacing traditional roles.

However, focusing solely on the jobs replaced paints an incomplete picture. The tech industry has created millions of jobs that didn't exist a few decades ago. App developers, data scientists, AI trainers, and user experience researchers are roles birthed by our modern technological landscape.

Furthermore, AI and automation often handle repetitive, mundane tasks, allowing human workers to focus on more creative, nuanced, and value-driven activities. Examples include: data entry and processing, clerical work, manufacturing and assembly, warehousing and logistics, inspections and quality control, legal research, and even medical diagnostics. Rather than replace human input, many technologies are designed to augment human capabilities, providing tools that enable us to work smarter and more efficiently.

Management < leadership

As you will see in a later chapter, the role of manager is being challenged. The old way of management via "butts in seats"—with employees expected to be at their desks, in company offices, as much as possible—is being replaced with leadership, which takes a different approach. Leadership is needed to guide workers in the conceptual age to move beyond production and productivity to effectiveness and aligned outcomes. More on this later.

Adaptability and continuous learning

The key to navigating the modern workplace landscape is adaptability. As certain roles become obsolete, the onus is on both individuals and institutions to embrace continuous learning. The future belongs to those who can learn, unlearn, and relearn. Futurist Alvin Toffler is often quoted from his 1970 book, *Future Shock*, about how businesses need to change and evolve or they will die.

This remains more true today than ever but, in the face of rapidly accelerating technology, businesses also have *The Innovator's Dilemma*, introduced by Harvard Professor Clayton Christensen. *The Innovator's Dilemma* explores how incumbent businesses fail to move fast enough to catch the next business wave because the existing business is performing so well. Think Kodak. They were the leaders in film and film paper. They even pioneered the digital camera. But the profits from film were so large, they failed to see the consumer demand change from taking pictures to capturing memories. More on the iPhone later.

Education systems must pivot from rote memorization to critical thinking, creativity, and emotional intelligence. Skills that make us inherently "human" will be at a premium, as these are the hardest for machines to replicate.

Companies will need to access learning spaces for employees to learn, unlearn, and relearn. Learning spaces are expensive and generally not used by one company daily. We are seeing the rise of flexible and agile workspaces that allow companies and employees to book space for any period of time, from one hour, to a day, week or even a month at a time.

CASE STUDY
CONVENE

Companies like Convene have emerged to provide first-class spaces and services for other companies looking to gather for a myriad of reasons, including education and training. Convene fills the gap between traditional office setups lacking meeting spaces and the unsuitability of hotel ballrooms for companies' daily use.

Founded in 2009, Convene is the largest single provider of dedicated meeting and event venues in North America and the United Kingdom. The network of thirty-nine locations across nine cities brings hospitality to traditional real estate.

Convene found the seam between traditional office setups and hotel offerings. The model addresses the need for collaborative workspaces beyond traditional offices not well served by office buildings or hotels alone.

Building owners benefit by generating income from rent and fees, offering world-class amenities and meeting spaces, driving higher foot traffic to the building, supporting other services, and leveraging Convene's operational expertise in hospitality to operate and market the space.

Convene customers benefit by having the flexibility of scheduling meetings in top-tier facilities without long-term commitments. Service levels, amenities, and food and beverage offerings match or exceed those of luxury hotels, but costs are lower for daily business use. In addition to leading-edge audio-visual and remote conferencing capabilities, Convene is also able to personalize meeting requirements and incorporate multiple locations within its networks.

Out with the old, in with the new

I often say to my adult children, "The work you will be doing in ten years likely doesn't exist today." There is a myriad of jobs, both blue-collar and white-collar, that will be displaced by technology and automation. There will be an emergence of even more jobs to design, prompt, calibrate, train, and oversee the technology in order to deliver effective results.

While some jobs, performed by humans, will not disappear completely, you can expect to see drastic reductions—along the lines of horse manure engineers, telephone switchboard operators, and gas station attendants. GenAI job replacement will likely center around work that involves:

- Repetitive or structured tasks, like data entry, bookkeeping, and so on

- Extracting patterns and insights from large amounts of data, like credit analysts, financial traders, actuaries, and medical diagnostics

- Language processing and generation, like copywriters, technical writers, translators, and receptionists

- Transportation and delivery, like truck drivers, delivery drivers, forklift operators, and robo-taxis

- Rote creativity, like graphic designers, composers, writers, and artists

So, what will arise in their place? New-collar jobs.

Former IBM CEO Ginni Rometty coined the phrase "new-collar jobs" in 2016. IBM was having a hard time filling cybersecurity jobs, partly because outdated criteria required that candidates have college degrees. "Because we over-credentialed for those cyber jobs, we were overlooking an entire pool of qualified, available candidates," Rometty wrote in an email, shared by Lora Kelley in her *New York Times* article titled "Wanted: 'New collar' workers".

Hiring managers are increasingly using skills-based filters on LinkedIn to find candidates, Kelley wrote in her article. In fact, she reported that, according to a LinkedIn spokesperson, 155 million users (seventeen per cent of LinkedIn's user base) don't have a four-year degree.

New-collar optimists acknowledge that new jobs supporting the accelerating world of technology will require advanced skills but not necessarily advanced degrees, especially in fields like artificial intelligence, cybersecurity, electric vehicles, and robotics.

Companies like Google understand the need to train employees in both basic and advanced areas. While both the private sector and universities advance upskilling and reskilling, there is a need for additional government intervention as well. The House of Representatives introduced versions of the New Collar Jobs Act in 2017, 2018, and 2021, but the legislation failed to pass. The bill would provide thirty billion dollars in federal grants to community colleges and training providers to expand programs in sectors like IT, advanced manufacturing, healthcare, and construction. The goal of the legislation was to help close America's skills gap by preparing an additional ten million skilled technicians, operators, and engineers over the next five years.

Why is this important? Promoting workforce readiness in technical fields and supplying talented personnel builds resilience across infrastructure, manufacturing, and technology. Over the next decade, there will be approximately 3.5 million unfilled manufacturing and infrastructure jobs due to lack of training, according to Deloitte. Currently, there are over 600,000 unfilled manufacturing jobs in the US while eighty per cent of manufacturers report difficulties in finding skilled workers, reports the National Association of Manufacturers. Over the next five years, US infrastructure projects are anticipated to create over 25,000 STEM related jobs each month. According to the U.S. Department of Commerce, current graduation rates will meet less than a third of demand.

A conservative estimate puts the annual cost of the manufacturing skills gap at 17.5 billion dollars due to lost revenue from unfilled positions, according to the American Society for Quality. This shortfall creates both an economic and national security threat. Key issues around national security include: supply chain vulnerabilities, degrading infrastructure (roads, bridges, and so on) economic stability, and emergency response readiness.

Enter Google Career Certificates. Amid the rapid changes in technology, and increasingly unaffordable college tuition, Google created professional certificates, offered online through Coursera for high-demand fields like IT support, data analytics, project management, and UX design. They generally take three to six months to complete.

Over 45,000 students have earned Google Career Certificates since their launch in 2018. The company reports graduates have a strong understanding of practical skills needed for entry-level roles. Certificates are affordable alternatives to degrees, costing forty-nine to ninety-nine dollars per month compared to 10,000 dollars to 30,000 dollars annually for in-state public college tuition.

By 2025, it's estimated over sixty per cent of jobs will require skills training beyond high school but not necessarily a four-year degree. Certificates provide critical mid-skills training.

Even established and credentialed employees need to hone their skills in the age of acceleration. It's truly a Red Queen moment. In Lewis Carroll's novel *Through the Looking-Glass*, (the sequel to *Alice's Adventures in Wonderland*), Alice encounters the Red Queen in Looking-Glass Land. Explaining the nature of Looking-Glass Land to Alice, the Queen says, "Now, here, you see, it takes all the running you can do, to keep in the same place."

The Red Queen phenomenon describes a situation in business where companies, like the Red Queen, must constantly run to stay in the same place. It's a metaphor for the dynamic and competitive nature of the business world where simply maintaining your current position requires constant adaptation and innovation. Getting ahead, creating differentiation, and accelerating in the age of acceleration is required more than ever to combat escalating competition. The need for agility—the ability to change and move quickly—is paramount.

Impact on the built environment

With new and emerging jobs popping up faster and faster, how might we think about work, the workplace experience, and the office asset class?

Job evolution and composition will invariably impact the built environment. We will need a more flexible and agile future in order to accommodate the rapid changes happening to businesses and the people working within them.

Oftentimes, companies open a new office with a ribbon-cutting ceremony. Traditionally, the ribbon cutting is a conclusion to a process. There is a party. The event is often telecast around the world to other offices. Speeches are made and people congratulate one another. There is a spirit of accomplishment and finality. Unfortunately, the ribbon cutting is not the end.

Ribbon cutting in the conceptual age is the start; the kickoff to an agile future of a particular space. The office design needs to incorporate as much flexibility and agility as possible. Office design needs to emulate the flexibility found in hotel meeting areas. Walls and furniture need to be movable, for example.

There is a big leap from ribbon cutting as end goal to starting line. Senior leadership will need to adapt a starting line mindset. Sensors and other IoT are needed to provide much-needed data about usage and effectiveness. As we explored the macro view of job change, we also see how corporate real estate departments will need to adapt and evolve.

The future rule of corporate real estate

The employee is the new office consumer. With agency, autonomy, and optionality, the consumer will vote with their feet regarding where and how they work. Traditional CRE departments are made up of real estate, lease administration, project management, and facilities management. More progressive CRE departments incorporate business intelligence and property technology. Some organizations have one leader overseeing the entire CRE department while others have separate reporting structures into finance and/or operations.

The increased acceleration of technology and work requires a new set of skills and approaches to maintain and optimize a global corporate real estate portfolio. There are opportunities to leverage GenAI and machine learning in order to maintain, organize, and query the millions of data points associated with a real estate portfolio. This holds true for building owners and occupiers.

In 2017, Hurricane Harvey struck south Texas as a Category 4, making landfall near the coastal city of Rockport and dumping over fifty inches of rain. Harvey caused catastrophic flooding and impacted the densely populated city of Houston. At the time, I was the head of real estate for Walgreens, which operates the largest pharmacy store chain in the country. Walgreens had over 100 stores in the storm's path; many were damaged and a handful were destroyed. The Walgreens real estate team needed to determine our rights under the casualty and restoration clauses. We needed to determine how exposed the company was in terms of rebuilding requirements. The potential financial impact to the company was as high as 100 million dollars. It took a team of eight people two weeks to scour through the myriad of physical leases. In today's world, with a proper GenAI and machine learning installation, the list and details would be generated in under fifteen seconds.

The Internet of Things was a wonderful technological addition to commercial real estate. But, just like in the case of Hurricane Harvey, the ability to query and quickly analyze data is hindered by outdated, time-consuming search methods. The amount of new data being generated each year increased from 1.2 zettabytes (one trillion gigabytes) in 2010 to 180 zettabytes in 2023, a 14,900 per cent increase. So, data and big data is not the driving force; insights from the data create the value. Data is like oil in the ground. It has value and potential energy. Unless—and until—it is extracted, refined, marketed, and sold, it remains just that: potential. Once processed, it moves from potential to kinetic.

The future of commercial real estate is less about data and more about insights. How to work smarter, not harder. How to access mass information via a keyboard query versus a manual search.

CHAPTER SUMMARY

The dialogue shouldn't be about "man versus machine." Instead, it should focus on how man and machine can coexist and collaborate. History has shown that job displacement due to technology is often a phase of transition. It's a period of adjustment that, while challenging, can lead to broader horizons if navigated with foresight, adaptability, and a commitment to lifelong learning. In the subsequent chapters, we'll delve into how these technological shifts are molding our present and shaping our future.

Technological evolution has dramatically impacted the who and where of working and shopping. Back in the mainframe era, knowledge workers were bound to their desks and desktops. Now, with the advent of spatial computing, we are entering a new era of "man and machine." Spatial computing is an emerging field that focuses on the interaction between humans, machines, and the physical environment. It encompasses a wide range of technologies, from augmented reality (AR), virtual reality (VR), and mixed reality (MR) along with the Internet of things.

Apple unveiled the Vision Pro in 2023, its highly anticipated entry into the AR/VR category. Consumers view through it, rather than at it, blending digital elements with your physical world. With Vision Pro, physical space becomes the canvas for apps, documents, video chats, and more. No need for keyboards or mouses. The Apple Vision Pro is shaping the interface. In short order, we will be looking at keyboards as interface as fondly as shag carpet from the 1970s. Add GenAI and quantum computing to the mix, and spatial computing will generate whole new experiences and roles.

Technological change has long created anxieties about jobs being replaced by automation. From the Luddites smashing mechanical looms to current fears about AI, concerns about job displacement persist. However, history shows that while some jobs fade, new ones emerge, often in greater numbers. The key is adaptability.

As innovations like manufacturing machinery and automobiles changed workplace and consumer demands, the demand for roles like blacksmiths declined but opportunities boomed in new areas. AI and modern technology can automate repetitive tasks but also augment human abilities and create new industries. Companies like Convene, providing flexible workspaces, are examples of this.

However, certain jobs are more vulnerable to replacement by intelligent automation doing tasks involving data processing, transportation, and rote creativity. This will displace many workers. Supporting job transitions through continuous learning, and developing complementary strengths suited to human talents, will be vital.

Physical spaces will also require flexibility to support rapidly evolving jobs. Ribbon cutting should signal a beginning, not an end point. Agile, easily reconfigurable office designs combined with utilization sensors will enable data-driven adaptations. Work is becoming more fluid rather than fixed.

Corporate real estate groups must also enhance skillsets in this climate. Adding competencies in business intelligence, workplace experience optimization, and change management, coupled with the use of proptech (property technology), will help firms address accelerating demand fluctuations.

The key throughout is recognizing jobs lost to technology while proactively gaining new opportunities. For workers and institutions, and the buildings they occupy, embracing agility, lifelong learning, and human-centered design is essential to thrive.

3

TECHNOLOGIES
OF THE FUTURE

*"Technology makes it possible to build things
that could not have been built before, but it does
not ensure that they will benefit humanity or
even that their benefits will outweigh their costs."*

YUVAL NOAH HARARI

A S THE PACE of technological advancement accelerates, so does its potential to shape our world in ways previously reserved for the realm of science fiction. Today, we find ourselves on the cusp of innovations that promise to redefine not only the way we work, live, and communicate but also the very essence of what it means to be human.

The ramifications for the built environment will be even more tectonic than we experienced in the first quarter of the twenty-first century. My friend, Tom Stat, is a polymath. He led IDEO's Chicago office for many years and has degrees in aerospace engineering, psychology, architecture, and business. In short, he's my Yoda. Tom likes to say, "The when, who, and where of work are critical ingredients of outcomes. Few people are focused on the 'how' and 'why' of work." We are on the doorstep of yet another extraordinary platform shift.

Why geek out in this book? Why go deep into technology? Simply put (and, in so doing, highlighting the overarching theme of this book), accelerating change in technology is transforming consumer behavior and having a profound impact on the built environment. Patterns of working and shopping are changing. Asset classes are at risk. Certain communities are more vulnerable and exposed. And if the rate of change up until now has been daunting, the next ten years will be mind-blowing.

Bill Gates captured it best when he said, "We always overestimate the change that will occur in the next two years and underestimate the change that will occur in the next ten. Don't let yourself be lulled into inaction." With that in mind, let's take a deeper look at the rise of GenAI and artificial general intelligence (AGI), the groundbreaking role of synthetic biology, and the coming quantum platform shift.

GenAI and the dawn of AGI

GenAI has rapidly evolved from simple, rule-based systems to sophisticated models capable of learning from vast datasets. Howard Gardner, American developmental psychologist, renowned for his theory of multiple intelligences, provides an important definition: "Intelligence is the ability to solve problems, or to create products, that are valued within one or more cultural settings."

The consumer needs to value the solution or the product. Based on the rate of adoption of various GenAI models, it would appear that we are moving quickly from innovation, through early adopter and into the early majority. ChatGPT 4, from OpenAI, reached 100 million users in just two months after its launch in November 2022. This makes it the fastest-growing consumer application in history. ChatGPT 4 acquired one million users just five days from launch. Compare this to Instagram and Netflix, which took two and a half months and three and a half years respectively to reach one million users.

There are two important definitions in the field of AI: narrow AI and general AI. David Kiron, in a 2017 *MIT Sloan Management Review* article titled "What Managers Need to Know About Artificial Intelligence", defines narrow AI as "a machine-based system designed to address a specific problem (such as playing Go or chess)". In contrast, general AI refers to machines with the ability to solve many different types of problems on their own, like humans can. To date, all applications of AI are examples of narrow AI. While general AI is currently a hot topic, it will likely take several decades to achieve true realization.

GenAI is a great example of how, as Bill Gates said, we overestimate change in the short term and underestimate change in the long term. It seems like everything happened all at once for the consumer yet technologists have been building the foundation for today's GenAI since the 1950s.

Alan Turing, eminent British mathematician and computer scientist, helped break the Nazi's Enigma code encryption, which dramatically impacted the Allied war effort. He was an early pioneer in artificial intelligence, programming language development, and hardware development. Turing further created the "Turing test" or "imitation game" to test whether machines could exhibit intelligent behavior indistinguishable from humans.

To date, no AI tool has passed the Turing test. Many experts believe AI could pass a "weak" version of the Turing test between 2029 and 2034. Most experts believe the median estimate for AI reaching a general level of intelligence indistinguishable from a human ranges from 2040 to 2045. At the time of writing, that's only sixteen years away. Quantum computing could accelerate development and deliver artificial general intelligence sooner.

The growth of GenAI

The early days of GenAI (2014 to 2020) saw limited mainstream consumer adoption. Neural network-driven GenAI remained mostly within the computer science community.

Companies like Synthesia and Anthropic (Anthropic's Claude is my favorite GenAI) began leveraging consumer use cases like synthetic media and conversational chatbots. These challenges were important because they were designed to connect people with computers so that—collectively—they act more intelligently than any person, group or computer has even done by itself before. Adoption was still largely limited to tech enthusiasts though.

In 2021, tools like Dall-E 2, Stable Diffusion, AI audio/video generation, and ChatGPT preview launched, showing remarkably good results on easily accessible platforms. Momentum was building in 2022, which saw rapid progress in natural language abilities with ChatGPT and image generation where non-tech users started playing with GenAI just for "fun." Microsoft and Google announced integrations into consumer products, signaling mainstream comfort with everyday usage.

As mentioned earlier, ChatGPT hit the 100 million user mark in only two months. Other AI platforms evolved, including Gemini for Bard from Google and sites like POE, which aggregate a whole selection of multimodal AI.

New technology can bring positive benefits for business and society, and offer advanced tools for those with nefarious intentions. In 2023, we saw Kendrick Lamar release a music video for a song titled "The Heart Part 5", which examines themes of race, identity, celebrity culture, and the state of America. The video contains deepfake technology, with Lamar's face morphing into those of public figures. Specific figures were chosen to represent specific themes or messages, including: Kanye West for mental health and the pressure of fame, Will Smith for Black masculinity and the cycle of violence, Kobe Bryant for legacy and the pursuit of greatness, Nipsey Hussle for entrepreneurship and social activism, O.J. Simpson for race, justice, and the American legal system, and Jussie Smollett for media manipulation and the exploitation of race.

Lamar's song made an impact. Considered one of the best songs of 2023, it reached the top ten on *Billboard*'s Hot 100 and won several Grammy Awards. It was also one of the most popular videos of the year, with over 100 million views on YouTube in its first week. I was one of the first viewers. I couldn't believe the seamless change from one man to another. The alarm bells started to sound. Going forward, how might deepfakes be used in the blood sport known as US politics? How will AI-generated content be identified? Would high school students ever have to write an original essay again?

This book will not tackle the ethical dilemma embedded in the dark side of GenAI. Suffice it to say, as discussed in the previous chapter, creative destruction will be at play. Old jobs will be sidelined in favor of new roles, like GenAI ethicists, prompt engineers, and a new breed of software engineers focused on driving the AI models to code rather than directly coding themselves.

Synthetic biology: crafting life

Moving from the digital realm to the organic, synthetic biology stands poised to revolutionize our world. This interdisciplinary field merges principles from biology and engineering, enabling scientists to "design" biological systems.

From creating bacteria that can break down plastic waste to engineering crops that can thrive in the harshest of climates, synthetic biology could offer solutions to some of the world's most pressing challenges. It promises medical breakthroughs, environmental solutions, and even the potential of life on other planets.

The Human Genome Project was officially launched in 1990 with the ambitious goal of sequencing all three billion base pairs in the human genome. It took almost fifteen years to announce the fully mapped genome, which was lauded as a major scientific milestone for genetics with immense ongoing impact. Finalized in 2005, the entire genome represents approximately 750 megabytes of data. To put the sheer size in context, it would take over 100 volumes of 800 pages each to capture the full sequence.

The acceleration of technology aided scientists in their pursuit of understanding such an enormous data set. It also cost a lot of money. Mapping the human genome cost over 100 million dollars. Today, you can sequence your own DNA for approximately 500 dollars.

Building off the shoulders of genome giants, American biochemist Jennifer Doudna started her pioneering work in gene editing around 2007. Along with collaborator Emmanuelle Charpentier, Doudna discovered the potential of CRISPR-Cas9 to be programmed to cut any DNA. The back story is fascinating. Doudna and Charpentier noticed that bacteria were immune to viruses, leading them to wonder why. They went on to discover that bacteria produces specialized enzymes (proteins) that, when they encounter virus DNA, cut the DNA in such a way as to render it innate. They replicated what the bacteria already knew how to do to engineer proteins that could basically perform surgery on DNA. Cas-9 is an enzyme that works like a pair of molecular scissors. They used the Cas-9 protein to do the cutting. "CRISPR" stands for "Clustered Regularly Interspaced Short Palindromic Repeats." You will not be quizzed on this!

CRISPR-Cas9 opened up a remarkable range of practical applications, giving scientists the ability to directly edit, remove or alter DNA sequences within living cells. The first major example was gene therapy focused on genetic diseases—like sickle cell anemia, muscular dystrophy, and Huntington's disease—by directly fixing underlying mutations in the DNA. The technology is being expanded into agriculture for crop improvement and livestock modification, drug development, and biofuels. Whole new extensions of bioscience are emerging. One of the epicenters of cell and gene therapy is in West Philadelphia, adjacent to Drexel University and the University of Pennsylvania, and is affectionately called Cellicon Valley.

In the shadows of a former GE Defense building, where bombs and buoy-driven torpedoes were designed to destroy property and take lives, companies are expanding with both lab and office space to prolong and improve life.

How important is this technology? Jennifer Doudna and Emmanuelle Charpentier were awarded the Nobel Prize in Chemistry in 2020. In addition to the advances in gene therapy, experts project that synthetic biology will also improve and prolong life in the areas of regenerative medicine, nutrition and health supplements, environmental health, and prosthetics and implants.

Companies like Elon Musk's Neuralink are looking to combine computing technology with biology. Neuralink aims to develop a brain-computer interface (BCI) technology called the "N1 Link" with the potential to revolutionize various industries. Potential applications include: medical (treating neurological disorders and mental health treatment), consumer (augmented reality, brain-controlled devices, and cognitive enhancement), and military (improved soldier performance, and brain-controlled weapons and systems). The market size for BCI businesses is projected to reach 3.7 billion dollars by 2027.

We are seeing the accelerating confluence of human and computer to advance all manners of society. That acceleration continues to roughly follow Moore's law, but things are about to change. Fast. My aforementioned friend, Tom Stat, cannot stop talking about his test-ride of the Apple Vision Pro and the spatial computing experience. The man/machine interface will continue to evolve, even if you don't want a chip in your head.

Quantum computing: the next leap

Classical computers (yes—we are going to start calling them classical), even the most advanced ones, operate on the principles of classical physics, utilizing bits as their basic unit of data, which can either be zeros or ones. Quantum computers, on the other hand, leverage the principles of quantum mechanics to perform computation. Quantum mechanics is a branch of physics that governs the behavior of matter and its interactions with energy at molecular, atomic, nuclear and even smaller microscopic levels. While classical computing relies on one of two states, zero or one, quantum computing can exist in superposition of two states (zero *and* one) simultaneously. This creates a quantum leap in computational power, as there is an exponential increase in representational capacity and speedup of certain quantum algorithms. In terms of leaps forward, qubits are exponentially more powerful than traditional bits.

With the addition of each qubit, computing power doubles. So, while twenty transistors (the base switch between ones and zeros in the classical computer) provides twenty times the computing power, twenty qubits represent one million times more power than one single qubit.

This property allows quantum computers to process a high number of possibilities simultaneously, making them immensely powerful for specific tasks like cryptography, optimization, and drug discovery. While still in their nascent stages, quantum computers have the potential to solve problems deemed unsolvable by today's standards. The human brain, or neural network, is the holy grail for scientists developing quantum computing.

Quantum computing can significantly enhance computational power and speed, enabling complex calculations and simulations that are currently unfeasible with classical computers. This could lead to breakthroughs in fields such as materials sciences, synthetic biology and drug discovery, and financial modeling. One of the biggest opportunities and threats involves information security. On one hand, quantum computing can potentially break traditional cryptographic algorithms that rely on the difficulty of factoring large numbers. On the other hand, quantum technologies can also provide new cryptographic techniques, which will enhance data protection. But existing cybersecurity, based on classical computers, will be instantly obsolete with the advent of quantum computing.

The development and adoption of quantum computing will create new job opportunities and change the skill requirements in the workforce. We can foresee an increase in demand for quantum physicists, computer scientists, and mathematicians and engineers with expertise in quantum algorithms and quantum information theory. Organizations will require professionals who can strategically apply quantum computing to drive innovation and optimization to solve complex and previously unsolvable problems.

Preparing for the quantum platform shift

When existing computing power increases by twenty times and then new computing power by *one million* times, you need to realize that this level of change has never been experienced in human history. The cascading effects in all realms of life will be profound. We see the early founding fathers of GenAI concerned about ethical considerations, safety and responsible usage, transparency, and global regulation. While many use nuclear weapons as an example of how we can regulate technology with existential potential, we must remember that, for the most part, nuclear weapons are in the hands of governments while AI tools are widely distributed and in the hands of individuals.

There is an arms race of a different sort in and around AI. Many companies are launching an AI division or spinoff. Other startups are adopting the .AI suffix in their company names and websites to ensure attachment and adjacency to the burgeoning area (in fact, my website is www.joebrady.ai). In terms of change and speed, this gold rush is just the beginning. Quite simply, quantum will bulldoze our old ways of doing things.

Darío Gil, director of IBM Research, expects the widespread impacts of quantum computing to be felt by the end of the decade. That's six years away at the time of writing.

Inspired by John F. Kennedy's call to land a man on the Moon by the end of the 1960s, Gil and IBM are advancing research and real-world application with partners like Cleveland Clinic, an academic medical center based in Cleveland, Ohio.

IBM and Cleveland Clinic established the Global Center for Pathogen Research and Human Health in 2021. The new center is exploring how innovative technologies like quantum computing could help tackle viral diseases or lead to new medical breakthroughs. An initial area of focus is examining how quantum computing could accelerate discovery of new treatments, vaccines or approaches for preventing viral pathogen transmission. Proteins change shape depending on what they are doing and what proteins they are doing it with. It's relatively opaque for leading physicians to observe and predict protein behavior with classical computers. There are computational limitations to view proteins in real time. Quantum is providing a glimpse into the "possible."

CHAPTER SUMMARY

This chapter provides a captivating and detailed look into revolutionary technologies that will change our lives and the way we work. The built environment will need to adapt and evolve to support these changes. Real estate will need more agility in the future to keep up.

Powerful generative AI models demonstrate the dawn of systems that can pass the "Turing test" and exhibit creativity, empathy, and intelligence alongside humans. Fortunately, the technological overlords are decades off. Meanwhile, tools like CRISPR enable the programming of life itself by editing DNA sequences. This merges digital abstraction with organic substance—two key pillars of future innovation.

Most monumental is the coming quantum era, representing a leap in computational power from bits to qubits. Exponential speeds of computation will help solve formerly intractable problems across drug discovery, finance security, and more.

With extraordinary change comes extraordinary responsibility. Guidelines for usage and advancement of these technologies must balance innovation with ethics and safety. Workforce skills must evolve, and workplaces need to evolve to support those changes. Workplace experience will be redefined with each platform shift. New roles will be needed to drive, guide, and manage organizations and businesses in the era of exponential acceleration. The "next" will become the "present" sooner than we think and there will be tremendous winners and losers, depending on the focus, preparation, agility, and curiosity needed to navigate the coming change.

4

THE EVOLUTION
OF RETAIL AND
CONSUMER PRIMACY

*"The consumer is king. If a retail business
isn't adapting to meet changing
consumer demands, expectations and
shopping behaviors, it won't survive for long."*

JEFF BEZOS

N THE SWEEPING panorama of technological progression, one sector stands out for its stark transformation over the past few decades: retail. Why is it important to study retail's history in the US? Because the office sector is having a retail moment. Brick-and-mortar stores, once bustling hubs of commerce, have seen an evolution that's both a lesson in adaptability and a testament to technology's ability to reshape industries. To understand the future of real estate and its interplay with technology, we must first examine the retail revolution's roots and ramifications. In the first half of this chapter, we do exactly that, starting with the origins of modern retail and what ensued (and why).

In the ever-evolving dance between consumers and businesses, a new trend has firmly planted its feet on the dance floor: consumer primacy. Historically, the retail industry led the charge in this arena, but the principles of consumer primacy are now echoing in the vast halls of the office real estate market. In the second half of this chapter, we delve into this concept, its origins, and its profound implications for the way we think about retail consumers and workspace consumers.

The good old-fashioned department store

In the US, department stores emerged in the mid-1800s, with early stores including Macy's, Marshall Field's, and Wanamaker's establishing large stores in cities like New York, Chicago, and Philadelphia. Department stores were created to offer a wide array of goods in one spot. Previously, shoppers had to visit multiple specialized stores to buy clothing, household goods, furniture, and more. Department stores consolidated those items under one roof and often became destinations in and of themselves, thanks to iconic designs by renowned architects like Daniel Burnham.

The post-World War Two period witnessed significant economic growth and prosperity in the United States. The G.I. Bill provided benefits to veterans, and a booming economy contributed to the rise of a prosperous middle class. The newfound affluence allowed many families to consider home ownership and a more comfortable lifestyle.

Historian James Truslow Adams first codified the concept of the American dream in his book *The Epic of America*. Adams defined the American dream as "that dream of a land in which life should be better and richer and fuller for everyone, with opportunity for each according to ability or achievement." For many people, the American dream manifested in the form of a house, a car, and a burgeoning consumer class. This notion was reinforced by television and films of that era, depicting idealized suburban life.

Suburbanization led to the expansion of department store chains and the anchoring of the first suburban mall in the US, Southdale Center (opened in 1956), in Edina, Minnesota. Southdale became a national symbol of car-centric, consumerist, post-war suburbia. Road systems were built, car culture dominated, housing growth followed, and adjacent retail was built supporting the trade around the mall. Other major metropolitan areas followed suit with their own malls, road systems, and housing developments.

Mall culture and category killers

As urban sprawl increased, the latter half of the twentieth century saw a shift toward suburban malls. Enclosed shopping centers became the epicenters of social and commercial life. From the 1960s to the 1990s, malls spread rapidly across America's suburbs, centered around the anchored department store with adjacent inline stores. Malls became community hubs and teen hangout spots. The number of enclosed malls increased from 300 in the late 1960s to over 1,000 in the 1980s. Today, there are fewer than 700 large shopping malls left.

Consumers flocked to malls and department stores in droves. Family traditions were made and repeated each year with pictures of the kids with Santa Claus and the Easter Bunny. Consumers went to the mall for back-to-school and Christmas shopping. Teenagers found a safe and well-lit place to hang out. Orange Julius, anyone?

At this point, "shop" was still a noun. It was a place consumers went to see, touch, try on, and buy merchandise.

Consumer primacy was minimal as the large players largely dictated fashion and availability. Consumers were reacting to the selection they were offered.

Then, in the 1960s and 1970s, we saw the emergence of big-box retailers like Walmart (1962), Target (1962), Kmart (1962), and Home Depot (1978). These retailers opened their doors and focused on discount prices, mass selection, and suburban footprints. But their impact was limited.

In the 1980s and 1990s, major big-box chains surged thanks to new store growth and expansion. They gained more scale, supply chain power, and shopper traffic, threatening department stores. More "category killers" emerged as well. Each individual department in a department store saw competitive threats from so-called specialized junior-anchor retailers. Examples included home furnishings and décor (Bed Bath & Beyond, Crate & Barrel, Pottery Barn), books, music, and entertainment (Barnes & Noble, Borders, Best Buy, Circuit City), office supplies (Staples, Office Depot), toys (Toys "R" Us, KB Toys), and specialty apparel (Gap, Abercrombie & Fitch, Victoria's Secret).

Consumers were getting more choice, and they started voting with their wallets, opting for specialized retailers rather than the generalist department stores struggling to compete across all categories. This fragmentation was a key factor in the department store decline over recent decades. Mall owners and department store operators either adapted to changing consumer demand or suffered.

E-commerce, Amazon, and the tipping point

Also in the 1990s, Jeff Bezos had an idea. In 1994, he founded online retailer Amazon, initially selling books before eventually marketing Amazon as the "everything store." In 1995,

Bezos sold his first book, *Fluid Concepts and Creative Analogies* by Douglas Hofstadter, via Amazon. In 1999, the company added toys, electronics, tools, and home improvement items to its marketplace. The same year, Bezos was named *Time* magazine's Person of the Year. In 2005, Amazon launched Amazon Prime, a subscription service offering free two-day shipping on millions of items.

Technological acceleration, driven by Moore's law, delivered more power to the hands of consumers. Better smartphones, faster connections, and intuitive apps helped move the primacy needle more in the consumer's favor.

There is no better illustration of these forces at work than the following graph of Amazon's revenue. In 1999, Amazon posted revenue of 1.6 billion dollars. By 2005, with the launch of Amazon Prime, revenue increased to 8.5 billion dollars. The exponential increase in Amazon's revenue impacted traditional brick-and-mortar retailers significantly.

Figure 5: Amazon Revenue, Annual ($ billions)

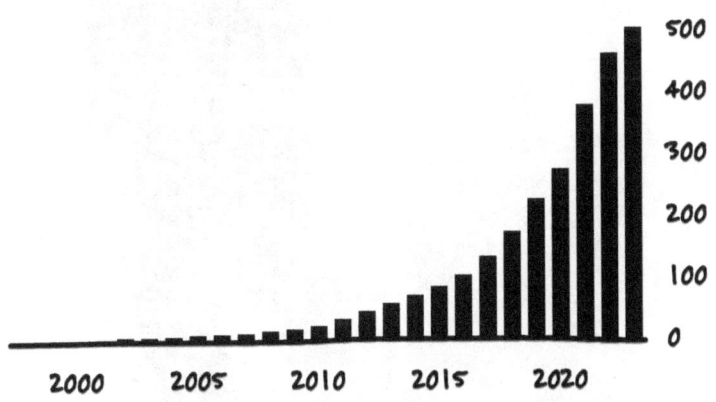

Source: Stock Analysis
(https://stockanalysis.com/stocks/amzn/revenue/)

In December 2019, driven by changes in consumer behavior, we saw a tipping point in retail. Using the traditional S-curve typically applied to technology, we saw online retail exceeding fifteen per cent of the retail sector for the first time. Amazon's revenue topped 280 billion dollars.

The growth curve is compelling, considering Jeff Bezos made headlines as *Time* magazine's Person of the Year in 1999, just at the beginning of Amazon's ascent. The caption on the front cover reads, "E-commerce is changing the way the world shops." There were many changes that year and no one could foresee how big e-commerce (or omnichannel) retail would become.

Figure 6: Time Person of the Year, 1999 – Jeff Bezos

Source: Time magazine

Increasingly, consumers are engaging in omnichannel retail. They are leveraging both physical retail stores and online digital channels, like websites and apps, for a seamless, consistent, informed shopping experience. They are leveraging capabilities like "buy online, pick up in-store", taking advantage of direct shipping from store to home, and engaging in returns across channels.

Omnichannel retail allowed the consumer to engage in a more kinetic manner, with the power to share, link to, comment on, and compare retail goods and services. The act of shopping became an evolved experience itself.

Figure 7: Tipping Point of Retail and the S-Curve

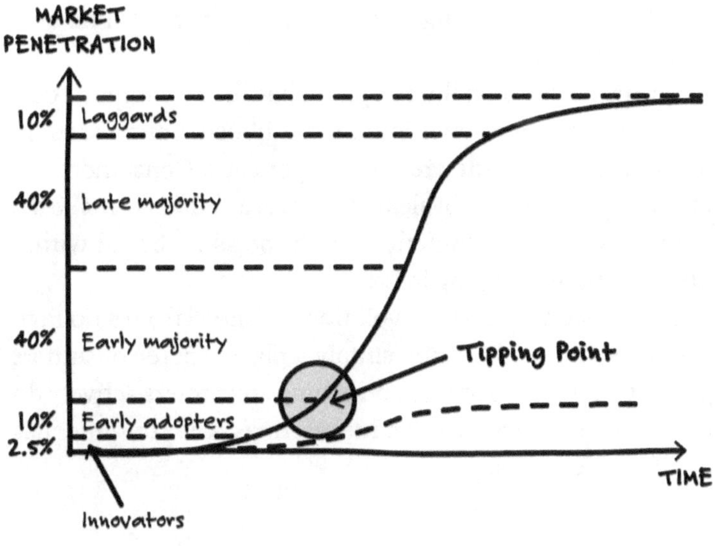

Source: The Business Growth Guys
(https://businessgrowthguys.com/tipping-point-of-retail-and-the-s-curve/)

Never has the consumer been more informed about, or attuned to, price, quality, and overall satisfaction. Customer reviews help steer consumers toward or away from certain products. Retailers have become increasingly invested in the data and insights business. Shared customer and inventory databases across different retail channels has connected inventory availability to consumer demand. Studying customer profiles and shopping behavior has helped dictate marketing, pricing, selection, and new physical store locations.

ICSC, formerly International Council of Shopping Centers, the member organization that promotes and elevates marketplaces and spaces where people shop, dine, work, play, and gather, conducted research on the impact of physical retail locations on online revenue. "The Halo Effect: How Bricks Impact Clicks", first published in 2018, revealed the opening of a retail store in a trade area created a thirty-seven per cent average gain in overall traffic on a retailer's website. Conversely, closing a store decreased web traffic by a similar amount.

In the latest installment published in December 2023, ICSC reported that opening a store boosts online sales in the surrounding trade area by 6.9 per cent. Consumers purchasing goods in a physical store were found to make 1.3 additional online interactions with the same brand within fifteen days of shopping in-store.

And so we've seen the evolution of "shop" from a noun to a verb. No longer is a shop simply a place where consumers go to buy things. "Shop" is something consumers actively do, irrespective of physical or online offerings. The consumer has finally gained primacy.

Consumer primacy in retail

Consumer primacy stems from a simple yet revolutionary idea: the consumer is king. The retail industry, faced with the rapid evolution of e-commerce and changing consumer behaviors, recognized that to stay relevant, it needed to place consumers at the heart of every decision.

This meant more than just offering products; it meant creating experiences tailored to individual needs, desires, and values. It was no longer about selling; it was about connecting. It was about experience. Physical stores needed to be "Instagrammable." Inventory needed to be new and fresh. As a result, we've seen the rise of "fast fashion" from retailers like Zara, H&M, Forever 21, and Uniqlo. While traditional apparel retail tends to look one or two seasons ahead and has an average of four inventory turns per year, fast fashion is known for refreshing inventory every two to four weeks and delivers over twenty inventory turns per year.

The internet and modern technology have also played pivotal roles in shifting the balance of power toward consumers. Online reviews, social media, and instant communication mean that consumers have both a voice and a platform. Their praises can elevate, and their critiques can cripple.

This newfound agency has given rise to the demand for transparency, authenticity, and personalization. A one-size-fits-all approach no longer cuts it.

"Agency, autonomy, optionality" is the new mantra:

Agency: Consumers want an active role in their experiences. They desire co-creation and collaboration.

Autonomy: The modern consumer values freedom and flexibility. They want to chart their paths, be it in shopping or in work.

Optionality: The power to choose, to have a range of options tailored to diverse needs and preferences, is paramount.

Different generations experience agency, autonomy, and optionality in different ways. For example, Baby Boomers still like to feel and touch merchandise. They are often dubious about giving their credit card details to online retail outlets. For many Baby Boomers, it has taken some prodding by the younger generations to shop online.

ICSC has provided further insights into consumer behavior by generation. While in-store is the preferred channel for all generations, a surprising finding is that Gen Z (aged eleven to twenty-six in 2023) prefer shopping in-store over older generations like Millennials and Gen X-ers. According to the ICSC, ninety-seven per cent of Gen Z shop at physical stores "thanks to the immediacy with which they can walk away with a product." In an interesting observation, Gen Z-ers are behaving like Boomers. Despite being digital natives, they are looking to try new products, ensure convenience, and enjoy the relationship-building aspect of in-store shopping.

Figure 8: Share of In-Store Revenue, by Generation

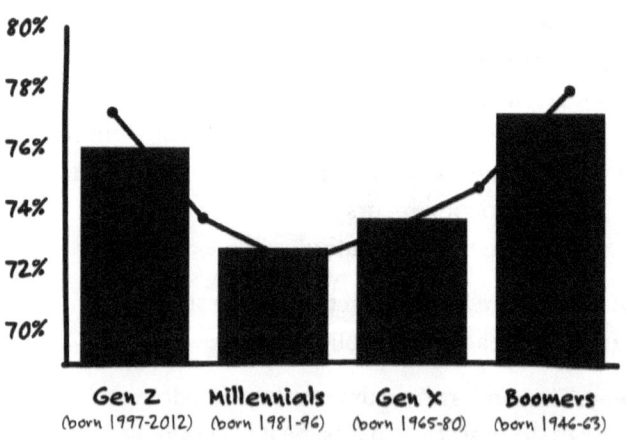

Source: International Council of Shopping Centers
(https://www.icsc.com/news-and-views/icsc-exchange/icsc-halo-effect-iii)

The rise of consumer primacy in retail follows the revenue curve for Amazon. Other online retailers certainly benefited from operating in an omnichannel fashion, but Amazon made the biggest impact. Consumer autonomy, or voting with your wallet, caused massive waves for both retailers and retail real estate.

Consumers were essentially voting on what was and what was not relevant. For retailers, inferior product, bad merchandising, and crowd-based negative sentiment could all lead to irrelevancy and demise.

The dustheap of history is littered with victims. While many failures were tied to excessive debt via leveraged buyouts (LBOs) and declining traffic in class B and class C malls, most fell victim to competition from online retailers. Mervyn's, Bonton, Borders, Sports Authority, Brookstone, Sharper Image (which turned out to be not that sharp), and RadioShack all collapsed or shrunk considerably. Some brands are seeing a second life online, like Toys "R" Us. For the most part, however, near-dead or declining retailers fell out of favor among consumers and were replaced. In 2020 alone, department stores JCPenney, Neiman Marcus, and Lord & Taylor all filed for bankruptcy, later emerging as smaller or digital-only players.

From a revenue perspective, we see the power of consumers voting with their wallets in the percentage of online versus in-store sales. E-commerce represented only five per cent of total retail sales in 2010, but grew steadily to reach fifteen per cent by 2015. During the pandemic, it jumped to sixteen per cent as stores were closed and consumers relied heavily on online shopping. Estimates for post-pandemic online sales range from twenty-five to thirty per cent.

Early in the rise of online shopping, naysayers were quick to call for the retail apocalypse and the death of brick and mortar. The consumer had other plans, however, and proved these predictions wrong. The clickbait portending the doom and gloom in an industry apparently sells newspapers and drives clicks, but it was just not true. The answer was more complicated and less reductive.

As you will see, the future of work is, likewise, more complicated and less reductive. What we do know is how consumers, of various generations, behaved in the face of change in the retail industry. We also know how retailers and property owners reacted (or not), and how that impacted the ability to win with agile and adapted practices.

The supposed death of the office is clickbait as well. There will always be a role for the office. It's just that "office" and "work" are forever decoupled. Like "shop" migrating from noun to verb, "work" has likewise evolved. From a place we went, to a thing we do, irrespective of location. This presents a more complicated challenge for leaders to assemble and engage employees. We will look at the role of leadership in a future chapter. In the meantime, what have we learned from retail?

Lessons for the real estate sector

The trajectory of the retail sector offers several takeaways:

Adapt or perish
Just as e-commerce reshaped retail, remote work and digitization will redefine traditional office spaces. The real estate industry must be agile in adapting to these changes. For occupiers of space, know your consumers. They are your employees. Track how they are using space. Offer a variety of spaces and see how they use them. How effective are the spaces? What works best for your employees' circumstances?

For owners of space, understand the game is changing rapidly. Understand the true economic buyer: the consumer.

The office game is moving from B2B (business-to-business) to B2B2C (business-to-business-to-consumer). There is a small minority of new and ultra-modern buildings, like One Vanderbilt in New York City, that will command the highest rents and traditional, long-term leases. But for every One Vanderbilt, there are hundreds of class B and class C buildings that need to compete.

Over seventy-five per cent of the office stock in New York City was built before the IBM mainframe. Meaning, it was built before 1964, the last year of the Baby Boomer generation. These buildings are over sixty years old and most likely approaching functional obsolescence compared with newer, more amenity-rich, energy-efficient, and competitive alternatives.

Some buildings are so functionally obsolete that replacement is inevitable. We are seeing former monocultures reshaped through public or private partnerships into healthy ecosystems of live, work, play.

CASE STUDY
DETROIT

Detroit native and billionaire businessman Dan Gilbert has made it his mission to spearhead the rebuilding and revitalization of downtown Detroit since moving the headquarters of his company, Quicken Loans, there in 2010. Gilbert has invested over 5.6 billion dollars into purchasing and renovating downtown buildings, including ones left vacant after businesses and residents fled the city during its decades-long decline stemming from the struggling auto industry.

Gilbert created Bedrock Detroit to carry out his vision for a vibrant live-work-play environment with walkability, culture, and innovative workspaces. Among his major projects include restoring historic structures like the Book Tower into residential apartments and retail space, building a unique "web of mobility" above the downtown area with the Detroit People Mover, and developing a visionary mixed-use skyscraper called Hudson's Site.

Gilbert has played an instrumental role in the rebirth of the city by spurring both business and residential investment in the downtown area. Over 100 companies have relocated to the revitalized business district under Gilbert's leadership. And with new restaurants, shops, event spaces, and residential buildings popping up, downtown Detroit is attracting thousands of young professionals and helping the city build momentum to get back on the map as an innovative metropolitan center. Critics say there is still work to do to reach blighted neighborhoods, but Gilbert has been widely praised for the remarkable progress made downtown so far.

Experiences matter

Just as retailers realized the unique value proposition of physical stores, real estate professionals must emphasize the experiential aspects that physical spaces offer, be it homes, offices, or leisure areas. Adaptability of office space and design should mimic retail by providing ever-changing configurations based on requirements, seasons, projects, and consumer needs.

Many retailers have created immersive, interactive, and memorable shopping environments that go beyond just selling products. How can these principles be applied to work and office space? Retail experiences helped differentiate retailers from their competition. The strong got stronger and the unimaginative suffered mightily. As the office asset class moves from B2B to B2B2C, differentiation will become a competitive advantage. As we know, employees (consumers) in the conceptual age don't work simply for a paycheck. They work for companies that offer purpose, great leadership, and life-enhancing experiences.

CASE STUDY
NORDSTROM LOCAL

Nordstrom, an American luxury department store, sought to get closer to customers and meet their needs outside of the traditional department store model. In 2016, it opened its first Nordstrom Local site in Los Angeles as a test concept. Locals were offered alteration services, style assistance, and shopping amenities in a smaller format without full inventory. Customers loved the convenience of trying on items and having them delivered to the store for pickup rather than shipped to their home. They also appreciated quick alterations done on the spot so new purchases could be worn right away.

Encouraged by the positive response, Nordstrom expanded the Local fleet and added new services like styling appointments. A typical visit now allows customers to meet with a stylist, have items shipped from any store for a fitting, and enjoy drinks or snacks as part of the experience. Customers searching for a specific item can get help tracking it down across the entire Nordstrom inventory.

Nordstrom Locals have proven so popular that the company aims to have 100 locations by 2025. Repeat visits are common as customers develop personal relationships with stylists. They appreciate the individualized attention and trust their stylist's eye for putting looks together. Nordstrom created a relaxed yet high-quality environment focused on great customer service, fulfilling a need beyond traditional shopping. This new localized concept has driven significant loyalty among new and existing Nordstrom customers.

One of the worst experiences for working people is the commute. For residents of Westchester County, New York, for example, the average commute time is over one hour each way, and the after-tax annual cost of commuting is over 8,000 dollars. Many people thought they were dismayed with their jobs before the pandemic, only to find, while working from home during the pandemic, that they actually like their jobs but hate their commute. How can companies decouple work from office and offer alternative venues for better employee experiences? In a B2B2C world, experience matters.

Integrate technology

One size fits one size. The best way that retailers found to individually target consumers was through leveraging data and analytics. Retailers use data to gain insights into costumer preferences and shopping habits, which informs decisions around inventory, store layouts, promotions, and more. In a similar vein, offices can use data and workforce analytics to understand employee needs, observe engagement, and evolve workflows and spaces to enhance the workplace experience.

Too many companies survey their employees and rely on that data to make strategic decisions. To quote James B. Duke Professor and behavioral economist Dan Ariely, "People are irrational—and predictably so." The problem with surveys is that humans often don't tell the truth and therefore the survey results are skewed. The key to capturing behavioral patterns is observation and there are many sources of technology that facilitate this. Of course, there are security and privacy concerns, but many companies have been able to anonymize data to show how people, not specific individuals, are using space.

CASE STUDY
XY SENSE

XY Sense was founded in 2016 to simplify the capture and application of workplace utilization data. XY Sense launched in July 2020, having spent more than three years in stealth mode perfecting its next-gen occupancy sensor and workplace analytics solutions.

XY Sense deploys sensors within office space, capturing anonymous sightings down to one foot (thirty centimeters) every two seconds with more than 98.5 per cent accuracy and no lag time. Real-time motion detection ensures richer vacancy and occupancy insights versus simple headcounts, passive infrared radars or Wi-Fi-based solutions.

XY Sense was deployed for a global bio-pharma in the US. In a new, experience-rich HQ office with over fifteen different office vignettes, it was determined in a matter of months that employees had a tendency to migrate to specific office schemes for work. It was also readily apparent, and supported by data, that other vignettes were not used at all. The company was able to remove the unwanted vignettes and replace them with the more popular layouts. This is real-time power from consumer primacy.

CHAPTER SUMMARY

Consumer primacy is reshaping the world around us. It's a call for businesses, industries, and sectors to listen, adapt, and co-create. In the realm of office real estate, it's an invitation to reimagine spaces not just as places of work, but as environments that empower, inspire, and evolve with their inhabitants.

The trajectory of retail over the past century epitomizes radical evolution. From the grandiose department stores of the early

1900s to today's experiential showrooms, omnichannel platforms, and demand-centric business models, the sector transformed in lockstep with socioeconomic forces and technological progress.

Several key themes emerge. Firstly, the consumer ultimately holds primacy in determining the success or failure of retail offerings. By voting with their wallets, consumers confer relevance. Secondly, adapting business models and physical spaces to align with consumer expectations and emerging channels becomes essential, not optional. Finally, experience triumphs over simple utility—retail must sell inspiration beyond products.

The parallels for the real estate sector are pronounced. While predictions of the wholesale "death of the office" are likely overstated, adapting workplace strategies and spaces to attract and engage today's talent is non-negotiable in an increasingly distributed world. The task of listening to user needs, integrating technology thoughtfully, and selling the unique experience of spaces matters more than ever.

Ultimately, the formula comes down to putting the end-user first and creating offerings flexible enough to meet rapidly evolving demands. In retail, this meant the consumer. In real estate, this means the occupant. Building owners and commercial occupiers need to view the occupant as consumer. The brands that internalize this notion will be best positioned to thrive amid continual change. Just as retail reinvented itself to align with empowered consumers, real estate must put flexible, experience-driven workplaces central to occupant needs at the core of strategy.

5

LESSONS FROM BEHAVIORAL ECONOMICS

"Traditional economists thought they were studying rational actors. What the behavioral economists had discovered was that even in very simple situations people were not acting rationally. They were acting like people."

MICHAEL LEWIS

HEN MICHAEL LEWIS penned *Moneyball* in 2003, it was more than just an exploration of the Oakland Athletics baseball team's unconventional strategy. It was a deep dive into the power of data analytics, the pitfalls of established norms, and the art of questioning the status quo. And while its primary focus was baseball, its lessons are universally applicable, including in the realms of consumer behavior and real estate. Just like work, baseball is played by people—and people are not always rational.

Michael Lewis wrote a successful book. I loved the book and the movie that followed. But the more interesting outcome from *Moneyball* was a review by two academic heavyweights that totally changed Lewis's thinking on the matter. In fact, it led to an entirely new and different book, titled *The Undoing Project*. More on that later. In this chapter, we'll discuss the impact of flawed human behavior in the workplace, and consider how we might do things differently as we venture further into the conceptual age.

The cost of refusing to unlearn and relearn

The 2003 review of *Moneyball* I referred to in the chapter introduction was written by behavioral economist Richard Thaler (University of Chicago) and legal scholar Cass Sunstein (Harvard Law School). Thaler was awarded the Nobel Prize in Economics in 2017, so the article drew Lewis's attention. While most reviews praised *Moneyball* as an engaging insight into the inner workings of baseball, Thaler and Sunstein waxed poetic about the work of two Israeli psychologists named Daniel Kahneman and Amos Tversky.

Thaler and Sunstein praised Lewis for adeptly explaining baseball's "peculiar economics" and detailing the analytics-focused approach of Oakland A's general manager, Billy Beane. They further highlighted that humans are biased and make decisions based on certain heuristics, or rules of thumb. Home-run hitters are great, right? Wrong (sort of). Statistically speaking, the probability of scoring a run increases dramatically if you simply get to first base compared to swinging for the fences.

By introducing Lewis to Kahneman and Tversky, Thaler and Sunstein added a new dimension to Lewis's thinking. Kahneman and Tversky are pioneers in the field of decision making and judgment, and considered founders in the field of behavioral economics. Their work shined a light on the fact that human decision making is prone to many types of bias, cognitive errors, and irrational behaviors.

In their 1979 paper titled "Prospect Theory: An Analysis of Decision Under Risk", Kahneman and Tversky presented a new model, explaining how people make decisions that involve risk and uncertainty. They introduced the concept of loss aversion. People are more motivated to avoid losses than achieve gains. The potential losses loom larger than the equivalent gains, at least psychologically.

You may be wondering how this is relevant.

During the pandemic, employees were offered an unexpected insight into a different kind of life/work balance. By working from home, people received raises by the simple nature of avoiding commuting and dining-out costs. They had time to exercise, read, and see their loved ones while still putting in more hours at their jobs. Some bad apples abused the opportunity, but there will always be slackers. The high performers thrived off this newfound agency and autonomy around their professional life.

Now, in the post-pandemic period, we see a proliferation of company mandates. In many cases, leadership is demanding employees' physical presence in the office to foster collaboration, culture, and other "c" words. Culture is built on trust and common values. Yet, from what I've seen, mandates erode trust. Mandates undermine trust and goodwill when they infringe on employee autonomy, discretion or input without strong justification or care for individual needs and impacts. Groups of employees from many companies have taken to social media and other online platforms to voice their opposition to a mandated physical presence in the office.

Even high-profile CEOs like Andy Jassy, who heads up Amazon, have issued return-to-office mandates. According to Jassy, the mandate decision was based on his gut feeling.

He called it a "judgment call" and suggested employees could leave the company if they didn't comply. If the intention was to gather people to build trust, community, camaraderie, and collaboration, the move backfired. Over 30,000 employees signed a petition opposing the three-day in-office mandate and over 16,000 employees joined a Slack channel, pushing back on it.

How did Jassy and other CEOs misjudge the reaction from employees? Why are CEOs hanging on to old, industrial-era constructs of work in the conceptual age? Michael Lewis found an unexpected insight that challenged him to unlearn and relearn about the book he already wrote. As previously mentioned, Richard Thaler and Cass Sunstein offered an alternative view of the baseball story. This prompted Lewis to write *The Undoing Project*, which is about Kahneman and Tversky.

Effectiveness surpasses productivity

The premise of *Moneyball* was straightforward yet radical: by relying on empirical data and statistics, the Oakland As could identify undervalued players and build a competitive team, even with a limited budget. This data-driven approach was in stark contrast to the traditional methods that relied on subjective judgments.

In the world of real estate, too, there are "established norms" rooted more in tradition than in objective analysis. For instance, the perceived value of a property based on its location, or its exterior aesthetics, might overshadow other critical, data-driven factors like energy efficiency, future urban development projections, or digital infrastructure.

The post-pandemic world creates another challenge for leaders leading their businesses and owners of commercial real estate navigating the Future of Work (FoW) landscape.

Historically, commercial real estate was based on the premise of "build it and they will come." The ribbon cutting was the end of the process. In the emerging consumer primacy world, the ribbon cutting is just the beginning. And in the conceptual world, employees/consumers are driving outcomes. Those outcomes have less to do with how many hours are worked and where. The biggest part of the challenge is measuring those outcomes and contributions, particularly in the context of the company's overall success. Effectiveness, rather than productivity, should be the key metric here:

Effectiveness > Productivity

Productivity is to home-run hitters as effectiveness is to getting to first base. Productivity is simply not the best metric to gauge engagement and performance in the conceptual age. Productivity is steeped in the industrial era of mass production where people worked in factories, inputs were delivered, humans operated machines with the inputs, and outputs were created. Labor productivity makes sense in an industrial context. In the keyboard economy, effectiveness is a better proxy.

As machines and artificial intelligence take over more routine and repetitive tasks, humans need to focus on higher-order conceptual skills: creativity, collaboration, synthesis, empathy, communication, and so on. Simply measuring how much output someone can produce is no longer the prime indicator of value. Rather, we need to assess one's ability to come up with innovative solutions, connect disparate ideas in new ways, understand diverse perspectives, and influence people through compelling storytelling. These skills allow people to augment technology rather than be replaced by it.

Moreover, in a world of exponential technological change, productivity gains become short-lived as automation and AI rapidly scale up output. Effectiveness, however, is a unique human capacity that counters the speed of machines. It demonstrates one's skill in leveraging technology to solve multidimensional problems, and provide meaning and clarity amid an overload of information. Maximizing these conceptual abilities is crucial for both individuals and organizations looking to maintain a competitive advantage now and in the future conceptual economy. In this way, Michael Lewis was ahead of his time in *Moneyball*—showing how effectiveness surpasses productivity, especially when the conditions around you accelerate faster than ever.

While productivity is focused on sheer throughput, effectiveness is aligned with a company's purpose and strategic initiatives. A worker could plow through hundreds of emails in their cubicle and claim victory. They processed scores and scores of emails and therefore they were being productive. But were they *effective*? Does the sheer nature of being busy equate to driving economic value?

We all know that coworker who has a tendency to sing their own praises and regularly announce to others how busy they are. Annoying, right? Well, these people are not only blowhards but purveyors in the productivity promise. "I'm busy, therefore I'm adding value." In truth, being busy in the keyboard economy, in the conceptual age, is no longer a competitive edge. In fact, you could argue such people are actually counterproductive to a company's overall purpose and strategic initiatives.

In contrast, effectiveness is essential to the FoW. Effectiveness revolves around solving complex, multidimensional problems with innovative solutions. It entails coming up with creative ideas, building connections between disparate interdisciplinary concepts, understanding diverse perspectives and needs, communicating compelling narratives, and influencing people through emotional intelligence. As routine, repetitive tasks get automated, the differentiator is exhibiting these conceptual abilities.

Measuring effectiveness means assessing the breadth of skills and aptitudes that allow an organization to thrive in the conceptual age. Metrics would track things like the number of new innovative services or products launched, the speed at which ideas get prototyped and tested, employee creativity and engagement survey scores, customer satisfaction and net promoter scores, cross-team collaboration levels, internal knowledge flows, and breadth of positive ecosystem impacts.

The most future-ready, economically healthy companies will reorient around maximizing organizational learning, decentralizing decision-making authority, incentivizing risk taking, and enabling people to build on each other's ideas. By assessing effectiveness related to these human-machine collaborative abilities, businesses can calibrate their preparedness for the exponential technological changes ahead. Those that merely maximize productivity will likely stagnate. Effectiveness defines conceptual age competitiveness.

Productivity paranoia

In 2022, Microsoft published a Work Trend Index Special Report: "Hybrid Work Is Just Work. Are We Doing It Wrong?" The study looked at how employees' schedules, productivity, and collaboration changed when remote work became the norm during the pandemic.

The study analyzed over 20,000 Microsoft employees in eleven countries, including managers, worldwide from March 2020 through March 2021. Key findings highlighted the paradox between management and workers. For example, eighty-seven per cent of workers felt productive working from home, while only twelve per cent of managers believed their employees were fully productive remotely. Usage of Microsoft Teams rose 153 per cent since the start of the pandemic, suggesting high activity levels. But there was no mention of how effective all those meetings were toward the company's overall mission. On another front, multitasking approached fifty per cent during those meetings. Yet managers reported lower levels of trust in remote teams.

If eighty-seven per cent of workers think they are working harder and are more productive yet eighty-eight per cent of bosses disagree, and don't trust workers to be productive unless they are in an office, we have a problem. The Dilbert management style of "butts in seats", inspired by the comic strip *Dilbert*, is not sustainable in the keyboard economy.

There are a number of implications that arise from the study:

- **Addressing the trust gap:** Building trust requires open communication, clear expectations, and performance indicators beyond physical presence.

- **Culture of asynchronous collaboration:** Tools and strategies should enable effective teamwork even when people are not online at the same time. As the conceptual age powers on and technology continues to accelerate, top talent will be more important than proximate talent.

- **Manager training:** To be fair, most managers in their managerial career are ill-prepared. They were likely strong frontline workers who were promoted. But that promotion generally does not come with adequate training. As previously discussed, the keyboard economy needs leaders, not managers. We know leadership is a learned skill. There are many roads and styles to leadership excellence.

- **Outcome focused:** Managers worry about how employees do things while leaders focus on outcomes. This is another succinct example of effectiveness surpassing productivity.

The nudge is mightier than the mandate

In the wake of the pandemic, the knee-jerk corporate reaction was to mandate employees back in office. While we certainly saw companies operating at opposite poles, the middle majority were muddled in uncertainty and confusion. The disconnect was highlighted in Microsoft's productivity paranoia, as highlighted in the previous section.

The big mandate makers included JPMorgan Chase, Goldman Sachs, Amazon, Disney, and all companies led by Elon Musk. In contrast, other companies, like banking group Citi, capitalized on employee frustration at other banks by offering a more hybrid and agile alternative working experience.

These mandates come at an interesting time. The war for talent is very real, yet it appears many companies haven't read the memo. Employees are viscerally reacting to mandates, despite many corporations applying a one-size-fits-all policy across the board. Mandates drive a behavioral reaction called reactance, which refers to the motivational reaction to rules, regulations or threats to freedom that cause a person to resist that imposition. Reactance leads to resistance and can propel people to do the opposite of what is expected. Return to Wok (RTO) mandates violate the agency, autonomy, and optionality that the consumer/employee experienced during the pandemic and perhaps even before it.

So, if not "brute force" via mandates, then what? Business leaders would do well to ask hard questions and study employee behavior to understand the internal and external factors that drive both decision making and effective work outcomes. Humans operate in unpredictable ways, not always practicing self-control, and are generally biased toward the past or the present rather than the future.

Leaders should be focusing on the behavioral science behind consumer behavior. In the emerging field of behavioral economics, we see choice architecture, also referred to as the "nudge", emerging as the key feature to help improve decision making. The father of the nudge is Richard Thaler, mentioned earlier. He coined the term "nudging", which refers to the use of positive reinforcement and indirect suggestion to overcome the inherent irrationality of human decision making. In their 2008 book titled *Nudge: The Final Edition*, Thaler and Sunstein define a nudge as "any aspect of the choice architecture that alters people's behavior in a predictable way without forbidding any options or significantly changing their economic incentives."

Choice architecture is a construct that is largely lacking in the corporate setting. But choice architecture has been proven to drive desired behavior and outcomes. Not by mandating and diminishing personal freedoms, but by creating alignment and incentives for desired behaviors. Successful nudges steer people toward good decision making, without ultimately depriving them of their freedom of choice.

The Dilbert manager, accustomed to gauging productivity by butts in seats, is fast becoming an extinct creature. But not fast enough. Their favorite weapon is the mandate. The irony is that mandates are issued in the name of culture and collaboration. Workplace culture is created by sharing similar values with an underpinning of trust. And what do mandates erode immediately? Trust.

Today's business climate needs leaders who understand an enlarging and evolving picture of how business is conducted in the age of acceleration. So, what are some examples of nudges? Nudge guidelines suggest that they should always be transparent, never misleading, easy to opt out of, and designed to improve the welfare of those being nudged. Some key areas for consideration in the working context include:

1   **Gather nudges:** Gathering is imperative but must be about purposeful presence over passive attendance. Why commute two to three hours per day just to sit in an office on Zoom calls? Leadership needs to do better. Onsite is the new offsite. Offsites always entail curated agendas, social time, food, and a desired outcome. So, too, should the onsite experience.

2   **Design nudges:** The office is not dead; cubicle farms are. Most office layouts are functionally obsolete. Employers need to quickly rethink design to enable gathering. The space needs to be as flexible and agile as the workforce requires. Future offices will have more similarities to hotels than traditional office spaces.

3   **Learning nudges:** We are in an age of acceleration. The rate of change OF the rate of change is moving faster than ever. Employers need to facilitate upskilling, reskilling, and continuous learning to accelerate growth.

4   **Life/work nudges:** Employees want a life outside of work. Working seventy to ninety hours per week might be seen as "productive" in terms of output, but is it effective? Life/work balance involves driving effectiveness, regardless of the amount of time worked. Examples include flexible meeting times to allow parents to take kids to school and pick them up, afternoon self-care time, and even sabbaticals.

5   **"Third place" nudges:** Former Starbucks CEO Howard Schultz popularized the term "third place" in relation to the coffeehouse chain, encouraging consumers to see it as a third place for work (after the office and home). Employers need to expand the concept and offer an ecosystem of places for employees to gather, work, learn, and be effective. More on this later.

6 **Effectiveness nudges:** Effectiveness focuses on doing the right things that align with company goals and priorities. Effective employees collaborate and communicate well with team members, adapt to change, can shift priorities, and deliver strategic objectives from leadership for clients, benefiting the overall enterprise. From providing healthy food and snacks, to standing desks, to automated reminders to take short breaks, nudges can encourage healthy habits among employees. Additional nudges can help employees selling and delivering products and services through default bundles, social proof points around best-selling items, and creating simplified MSA (master service agreement) documents that make the company easy to do business with.

7 **Intramural nudges:** Part of purposeful presence is gathering for team sports and games. We know the impact of intramurals in college settings. Teams competing in friendly matches, from basketball to trivia, help create esprit de corps, drive higher engagement, and lead to more effective work-related activities.

8 **Leadership nudges:** Leaders need to lead, not just manage. Management in the conceptual age is being heavily challenged. Management tends to micromanage time, activity, and production. Leadership sets the purpose and strategic initiatives, and promotes behaviors supporting both of those. Three examples of leadership nudges include open communication and feedback, promoting a growth mindset and continuous learning, and fostering collaboration and teamwork. The leader needs to curate more than in the past and certainly lead by example.

9 **Mentorship nudges:** Employers need to formalize the mentorship nudge. They can easily tie in previously mentioned nudges, like gather, life/work, intramural, and so

on. Having formal alignment between mentor and mentee can help smooth the uncertainty and volatility in today's work environment.

10 **Wellness nudges:** There needs to be more attention on getting and staying healthy versus fixing what's broken. Healthy employees are more effective employees. The top three wellness areas of sleep, exercise, and nutrition need to be incorporated into employer/employee engagements. Consider subtle rewards for group exercise during lunch hour, for example, and offering healthy snack alternatives.

Nudges, by no means, replace overarching meaning and purpose—especially in a work setting. Simon Sinek, in his book and TED Talk, both titled *Start with Why*, explains that people and organizations that excel are those with a fundamental "why". That is, a core purpose, cause or belief. Companies and people with a clear why inspire trust and loyalty because they believe in something beyond themselves or their products or services. Nudges are intended to support and amplify the why. Without the why, nudges have little impact.

CHAPTER SUMMARY

Michael Lewis's book *Moneyball* was ahead of its time. While the book was primarily about baseball analytics, it offered broader lessons about that the flawed nature of human decision making, which is irrational at times and prone to cognitive errors.

Moneyball highlights the value of embracing change, the importance of questioning established norms, and the power of data-driven decision making. In the fast-evolving world of real estate, where technology is rapidly reshaping consumer expectations and industry practices, these lessons are invaluable.

Just as sabermetrics transformed baseball, a data-driven, behaviorally informed approach can revolutionize the real estate industry. It's not about discarding traditional wisdom but enhancing it with modern insights, ensuring that every decision, whether it's buying, selling, or developing, is rooted in a deep understanding of both data and human behavior.

In the new conceptual age of work, companies need to move beyond outdated metrics like productivity and "butts in seats." Effectiveness, focused on conceptual skills like creativity, collaboration, and solving complex problems, is more important. Nudges based on behavioral science can influence behaviors more successfully than mandates, which often backfire.

For organizations to thrive, they must understand these behavioral insights. Companies should hire more behavioral scientists and choice architects to help design policies and environments. This will require assessing new metrics around outcomes, trust, learning, and organizational effectiveness rather than just individual outputs. As jobs change rapidly, continuous learning also needs to be formally supported through nudges.

Overall, applying lessons from behavioral economics can help transition companies to more human-centered, future-ready models. Nudges customized using choice architecture principles may be able to facilitate optimal behaviors relating to areas like hybrid work, wellness, mentorship, and leadership development better than blunt mandates can. Both traditional architecture and management are being heavily challenged in the new conceptual workplace.

6

THE NEXT FRONTIER OF OFFICE REAL ESTATE

"The future is already here—
it's just not evenly distributed."
WILLIAM GIBSON

AS THE LANDSCAPE of work undergoes seismic shifts, office real estate stands at a transformative crossroads. Just as our ancestors evolved from nomadic lifestyles to settled agrarian communities, the nature of "workspaces" is undergoing its own evolution, driven by technological advances and a renewed understanding of human needs.

Post-pandemic, we are seeing increasingly that "work" and "office" are two separate ideas. The office asset class represents three trillion dollars in the US economy. Upwards of fifty per cent of existing leases will expire by the end of 2025, and seventy-five per cent by the end of 2027. There will be a reckoning around renewals, size of renewals, and net new absorption based on technological and consumer behavior changes. Some predict that the reckoning will be like a slow-moving car crash. We see it coming but can do little to prevent the oncoming collision.

There will be multiple factors that play into how the office asset class will adapt and evolve over the next several years. As previously stated, changes in technology and changes in the rate of change will play a big role. If your business is changing at a frequency of six months, how willing are you to sign a long-term (ten-year) lease for real estate?

We are even seeing the indiscriminate use of a problematic phrase: "return to work." This is anachronistic and wrong-headed, as it implies that employees were not working during the pandemic. In fact, the opposite is true.

As discussed in the previous chapter, in 2022, Microsoft released data from an internal study looking at the productivity impacts of remote and hybrid work. Employees reported working harder, putting in longer hours, and replacing wasted commuting time with more "up time" on their work tasks. So, why the proliferation of the phrase "return to work"? Whatever the reason, one thing is for sure: words are powerful, and managers and leaders need to choose their words carefully. After all, the consumer is king and work in the age of acceleration is evolving, just not as quickly as technology.

In this chapter, we'll take a look at the corporate boom of the twentieth century, the rise of remote work and its impact, the role of the physical office in the twenty-first century, and consumer primacy in office real estate.

The corporate boom of the 20th century

In the mid-twentieth century, as businesses burgeoned, the need for administrative, financial, and managerial roles grew. Skyscrapers and office buildings began to define city skylines. In the aftermath of the Second World War, wartime technological advances began to influence skyscraper development. Advances in lightweight steel production, high-strength alloys, and elevator speed enabled taller buildings. During this time, the first "glass curtain wall" skyscrapers emerged.

In the 1960s, structural frameworks shifted from dense steel to lighter perimeter framing. Innovations like elevating zoning patterns, improved heating, ventilation, and air conditioning (HVAC), and electrical systems enabled taller towers with more usable space.

Built on bedrock along Lake Michigan, Chicago's John Hancock Center pioneered the mixed-use skyscraper, topping out at ninety-five floors above ground level. Developers combined offices, residential areas, shopping precincts, and restaurants. The world-famous Signature Room on the ninety-fifth allowed visitors to see three US states when the weather conditions allowed. Developers built a town square on the forty-seventh floor to service the 300 condos from floors forty-seven to ninety-two. Complete with a pool, grocery store, post office, and dry cleaning business, the town square was replicated at over 500 feet above street level.

The corner office

For a generation of people, the corner office represented professional attainment. The top of the mountain. "I've made it!" But getting there was difficult.

When I first started work after completing graduate school in 1990, I was a real estate corporate finance associate at First Chicago (now part of JPMorgan CHASE). The headquarters were located at One First National Plaza, at the exact center of the Loop in Chicago. The real estate team was based on the thirteenth floor of the sixty-floor tower. The big hitters had offices along the glass line. The really big hitters had the corner offices.

The lowly corporate finance associates were distributed on the floor at assigned desks. No partitions. No separations. Just a desk with a phone and a desktop computer. It really was open plan. You could hear multiple phone conversations. The mid-level bosses could easily peer out of their tchotchke-filled offices, with motivational posters on the walls, and determine who was being "productive" and who was not. Meeting rooms were at a minimum. It was essentially a factory floor with computers.

The corner office was viewed by **Baby Boomers** (born between 1946 and 1964) as a sign of success, status, and prestige. However, **Generation X** (born between 1965 and 1980) started having a less than glorious view of the corner office. This group tends to be more pragmatic and focused on results. While they may appreciate the perks that come with a corner office, like better views, privacy, and more space to house your tchotchkes, they are likely to value individual contributions and achievements over hierarchical symbols.

Millennials (born between 1982 and 1996) prioritize collaboration and flexible work environments over hierarchical structures. The emphasis is on open communication and teamwork rather than individual offices. As a result, Millennials are interested in redesigning office space to allow formal and informal meetings along the window lines. The views are no longer the providence of the big hitters.

Generation Z (born between 1997 and 2012) is generally considered the first digitally native generation. Gen Z grew up in an environment where digital technologies, particularly the internet and smartphones, were prevalent from an early age. The explosion of social media and other online communications occurred during Gen Z's maturation. They have never known a world without the internet and widespread digital connectivity. For Gen Z, the traditional office, let alone the corner office, can feel like a jail. They don't want to be segregated from their teams. Key attributes like global connectivity, diversity and inclusion, and environmental consciousness add to the opposition of the corner office.

Cubicle culture

Introduced in the late 1960s, the original intention of the office cubicle was to promote collaboration and flexibility. However, class warfare between the offices and cubicles was palpable. In the 1970s and 1980s, companies sought cost-effective ways to maximize office space. Cubicles were considered a modular and efficient approach to office design. The cubicle jumped the shark in the late 1990s. It went from being new and innovative to soul-sucking and demoralizing.

Employees found solace in third places, as mentioned in the previous chapter. In 1990, Starbucks had 165 coffee shops, all clustered in the western United States. By 2000, the company operated over 3,500 coffee shops across the US, Canada, and thirty-four other countries.

In 1999, Mike Judge (of *Beavis and Butt-Head* fame) wrote and directed *Office Space*. In the movie, Judge satirizes office culture and the frustrations of working in a corporate environment. Anyone who has ever worked in a large office for an intellectually lazy middle manager like Bill Lumbergh (played by Gary Cole) knows the agony of enduring the indignities of the cubicle farm.

In response to criticisms, office designs began to shift. The "cubicle farm" label was associated with a cultural perception of cubicles as soulless and oppressive. Gen X tolerated cubicles. Millennials demanded better.

As technological acceleration continues to change consumer behavior, we have **Generation Alpha** (born between 2010 and 2025) preparing to enter the workforce in the next five years. Gen Alpha are the children of Millennials. Their educational experience is different from that of almost any other generation given the lasting impact of the pandemic.

It will be vitally important to observe the emerging characteristics of this generation. From a technology perspective,

Alphas are demonstrably digitally native, yet they are emerging in an increasingly polarized world. Many of the jobs Alphas will be performing don't exist today. They will be the beneficiaries of some of the biggest technological breakthroughs, including quantum computing, and they will likely be the most agile generation the world has ever known. They will have to be.

The rise of remote work and life/work balance

Few could have predicted that a pandemic would become the modern era's most significant workplace disrupter. COVID-19 wasn't just a health crisis; it was a tectonic shift leading to rapid changes in office real estate. Jobs that companies never thought could be done remotely *were* done remotely— virtually overnight. The residential internet infrastructure supported the largest migration from office to home usage without a glitch. Cybersecurity, usually a blank-check line item, held firm. No breaches were reported that were directly attributed to working from home (WFH).

Quarantines and lockdowns meant traditional offices were no longer accessible. Businesses had to pivot overnight, adopting tools and technologies to facilitate remote work. What was once a perk became a necessity.

Zoom was founded in 2011 by Eric Yuan, a former Cisco executive, with the goal of creating a more user-friendly and reliable video conferencing platform. Zoom officially launched its service in January 2013. From 2013 to 2019, Zoom gained popularity for ease of use, reliability, and features such as high-quality video and screen sharing. Zoom became a public company in April 2019. Then, during the pandemic, Zoom experienced explosive growth. Friday afternoon virtual happy hours became the rage. Curated cocktails and games, like pub quizzes, were arranged. And companies were scheduling meetings as well. There was no choice but to engage via Zoom or other video conferencing technologies like Google Meet and Microsoft Teams.

During the pandemic, there was an ongoing prognostication about the "official" return-to-work date. While many thought it would happen following Labor Day 2021, the mutating virus had another agenda. False starts continued and, as a result, many workers began to push back against the return-to-work notion. More progressive and enlightened conversations starting arising around the FoW and the RTO concept.

In March 2023, *The New York Times* ran an article titled "Golf at 3 p.m. Thursday? Sure, It's the Afternoon Fun Economy." The article's author, Emma Goldberg, cites research and statistics about post-pandemic hybrid workers taking advantage of daylight hours to take care of personal needs (think hair, nails, yoga) and engage in leisure activities, like golf and tennis. Stanford Professor Nicholas Bloom has dubbed the phenomenon "the student economy." For many people, it's not a stretch to remember the student lifestyle—going to class in the morning, having lunch, then dedicating the afternoon to personal pursuits like varsity sports, intramurals, theater, and other extracurriculars. But, after dinner on a school night, once the sun has gone down, where do students usually go? To the library for a number of hours of study.

This portends an inversion of the work/life balance to life/work balance. Particularly in the conceptual age in the keyboard economy, we value outcomes over volume of work. Productivity tends to be tied to the latter. How many emails did you send? How many pages are in the PowerPoint deck?

Productivity is nebulous and has never been properly measured or tracked. In contrast, effectiveness, as previously discussed, means contributing to the overall success of a business or enterprise.

Reevaluating the role of the traditional office

As months turned into a year and then more, a realization dawned. Not only was remote work feasible, but it also offered several advantages—flexibility, improved life-work balance, and, in many cases, increased productivity. This prompted a pressing question: what is the role of a physical office? Here are some thoughts:

Hybrid models: Mirroring the omnichannel approach in retail, the future of work is likely to be hybrid—a blend of remote and in-office days tailored to individual roles and preferences.

Repurposing and resilience: Following in the footsteps of some retail spaces, which have transformed into experiential centers or community hubs, underutilized office spaces might find new purposes. From coworking hubs to innovation centers, the possibilities are vast.

Experiential workspaces: Just as modern retail spaces have shifted toward providing experiences, future offices might be less about providing a desk and more about offering an environment that fosters collaboration, creativity, and company culture. Think more of a four-star hotel lobby than a cubicle farm.

Consumer primacy in office real estate

Much like the retail industry, which had to rethink its strategies in the face of e-commerce, office real estate now faces its moment of reckoning. With the rise of remote work, flexible schedules, and the gig economy, today's workers are, in many ways, the consumers of the office real estate world. And they're demanding change.

Gone are the days when cubicles and rigid nine-to-five schedules dominated the landscape. Modern workers want spaces that feel inclusive and inspiring, and prioritize wellbeing. They want the freedom to choose where, when, and how they work. The principles of agency, autonomy, and optionality now resonate in the walls of office buildings. Coworking spaces, hybrid models, and wellness-focused amenities are all responses to these demands.

CASE STUDY
FULTON MARKET

Once Chicago's meatpacking district, Fulton Market has transformed into a thriving commercial and culinary destination. Located a few miles west of the Loop, Fulton Market benefited from being more of a mixed-use neighborhood prior to the pandemic. It already had densely populated residential high-rises and condos in addition to shops, restaurants, and office space. When remote work took hold during COVID, knowledge workers did not flee Fulton Market to the same extent as the Loop since live-work amenities allowed people to stay. Meanwhile, the Loop saw severe vacancies as offices sat empty. Fulton Market's diversity in uses, residents, and activities meant businesses could still find customers and foot traffic even if offices emptied.

As the Loop continued to struggle post-pandemic with high vacancy rates, Fulton Market saw continued investment and expansion. Tech companies and financial firms began relocating offices to inhabit the growing number of new commercial high-rises sprouting up among Fulton Market's warehouse architecture. Meanwhile, the lively culinary scene anchored by quality restaurants kept fueling vibrancy. On weekends, the Fulton Market area regularly tops lists as one of the most popular places in Chicago for socializing and live music. Having evolved as a more mixed and dynamic district, Fulton Market now rivals the Loop as a destination for both work and play.

The divergence between these two areas underscores how the Loop's former dominance as Chicago's monoculture business hub left it highly vulnerable to disruption. As companies and workers now have more flexibility in terms of where they are located, areas like Fulton Market have emerged as thriving business districts that could eventually surpass the primacy of the traditional downtown core. The future likely belongs to those urban cores better adapted to changing lifestyles through rich live-work-play integrations.

Fulton Market, and its evolving BBD, is a great examples of a district. Districts are emerging across the US, often replacing the old mall experience. Districts often sit at the confluence of sports, entertainment, and retail, with supporting hotel and residential developments. These environments allow for more meaningful, immersive, and social experiences. They are the most Instagrammable of places.

A great example of the district concept is Jerry World. Also known as The Star, in 1999 Dallas Cowboys owner Jerry Jones acquired 230 acres in Frisco, Texas for a new Cowboys headquarters and practice complex. In order to support the live/work/play ecosystem, the complex is now home to 2.5 million square feet of retail, dozens of hotels with over 4,000 rooms, tens of thousands of new housing units, and over eight million square feet of class A office space. Healthcare providers have also opened in Frisco to service the growing population, skyrocketing from 30,000 to 200,000 people.

CHAPTER SUMMARY

The pandemic ushered in a new era of hybrid work arrangements that combine aspects of remote work with time spent in a central office or workplace. By necessity, many employees transitioned to working from home fulltime during lockdowns. However, organizations soon learned that remote work had some unexpected benefits in addition to drawbacks. Surveys found that most workers enjoyed the flexibility and improved work-life balance that came with working remotely at least some of the time. At the same time, managers realized productivity didn't necessarily suffer and that face-to-face collaboration could still happen effectively through videoconferencing.

As restrictions eased, companies began piloting hybrid models that allowed a balance of remote and in-office work. Common hybrid setups required employees to come to the office only a few days per week, with flexibility otherwise. Core "collaboration days" were scheduled for meetings and interactive projects while "heads-down" work could often get done remotely. Teams experimented with different rotational schedules tailored to their needs. The hybrid model offered organizations a middle ground that maximized both flexibility and opportunities for in-person connection.

Implementing an effective hybrid model requires thoughtful planning around workplace usage and employee experience. Issues like facilitating impromptu collaboration, dividing office space, updating technologies, revising performance metrics, and maintaining company culture all need consideration. Iterative pilots and feedback are important to identify what works best for individual company norms. When well-designed, hybrid policies can improve recruitment and retention in a post-pandemic talent market that demands flexibility.

Research from a well-known media company and a leading architecture firm, studying the future of work, concluded that serendipitous, accidental, unplanned, unintended, and sometimes even voyeuristic interactions between unlike, unknown, and often competing workers had far greater value with regard to outcomes, effectiveness, and broadening perspectives compared with traditionally purposeful, defined, and organizationally prescribed interactions. In short, we need to leave room for the magic to happen. Just like helicopter parents can hinder their children's development, helicopter managers can't—and shouldn't—dictate every interaction between employees.

Overall, the hybrid work model looks set to become a permanent fixture for the vast majority of office-based companies going forward. With continued refinement, it offers a highly effective new paradigm balancing the preferences of employers and employees in contemporary work environments. We'll discuss the hybrid work model in more detail in the next chapter.

7

THE HYBRID
WORK MODEL

*"Done right, hybrid work can give dispersed teams
a greater sense of autonomy while still fostering
synchronous collaboration. It's about
maximizing human potential through flexibility."*

REID HOFFMAN

A S I CONTINUE to emphasize, hybrid work and omnichannel retail are two sides of the same coin. The common denominator in both cases is the consumer. Consumers are human and have different motivations, wants, and needs. As we've seen in the retail industry, failure to design, plan, and execute properly could lead to irrelevance. Irrelevance is an existential threat. Many subpar retailers and inferior malls found that out the hard way.

The big challenge is for corporate occupiers and building owners to adapt and evolve their thinking and execution with a consumer-first mentality. While many companies put their shareholders first, the leading companies put their employees first. If the employees are taken care of, the shareholders will benefit.

In this chapter, we identify three intrinsic motivations of employees and consumers alike, and why the hybrid work model is becoming increasingly attractive as a result. But first, let's explore some of the ways in which retail brands are redefining the retail experience—and what office real estate might learn from this as it also seeks to reinvent itself.

Hybrid retailers are winning the game

In the early days of the retail omnichannel movement, pundits and headlines screamed about the death of brick and mortar. Humans never had to leave their houses again. Everything and anything could be purchased from, and shipped to, our homes. This dystopian future was best illustrated by Pixar in the film *WALL-E*, featuring morbidly obese people using so-called hover-chairs instead of walking. All consumers had to do was sit back (and take big gulps from oversized drinking cups).

Fortunately, all the hype was just that. Omnichannel did not portend the death of brick and mortar. In fact, as discussed previously, retailers actually saw online sales increase in markets where new brick-and-mortar stores opened. Conversely, the online sales dropped when physical stores closed. As you already know from Chapter 4, according to research conducted by the ICSC, opening a physical store increases online sales by 6.9 per cent. Conversely, closing a store has an even greater negative impact on adjacent online sales, resulting in a drop of 11.5 per cent.

Leading retailers understand that consumers are looking for a wholistic shopping experience and a more meaningful relationship with brands. As a result, retailers are leveraging technology to track and understand consumer behavior. They are rapidly testing ideas that enhance the relationship between consumer and brand.

Many retailers have developed zeal-like followings from consumers who value the company's purpose. We see companies like Apple, Tesla, Trader Joe's, and Starbucks—all of which have strong brands and very loyal customers.

One of my favorite companies is Patagonia. Founded in 1973 by Yvon Chouinard, the company origin stems from Chouinard's work of selling mountain climbing gear that he made himself. We know Patagonia by the ubiquitous "better sweater" vests adorned by midtown bros, weekend warriors, and hardcore outdoor enthusiasts alike. In 2022, Chouinard decided to give away the family's ownership stake (valued at three billion dollars) into a specially constructed NGO entity called the Patagonia Purpose Trust. Chouinard was proud to announce that "Earth" was the biggest shareholder of Patagonia. Its sales continue to climb, and it remains a shining example of a purpose-driven retailer that has attracted a zealous following.

CASE STUDY
WARBY PARKER

Warby Parker was founded in 2010 by Dave Gilboa and Neil Blumenthal while they were students at Wharton's MBA program. Their idea started with a problem: glasses were too expensive. As it turned out, the existing market leaders enjoyed oligopolistic power, with Luxottica controlling over seventy per cent of the eyewear market.

Warby Parker launched exclusively as an online retailer, selling frames for ninety-five dollars and allowing consumers to try up to five different frames at home. The direct to consumer (DTC) approach allowed the company to keep costs low, while word of mouth helped grow the brand.

In 2013, just three years after launching, Warby Parker opened the first physical store in New York City. Since then, the company has gone public at a valuation of over six billion dollars and now has over 220 stores in thirty-nine states.

Initially, Luxottica largely dismissed Warby Parker, seeing it as a small, online-only startup that posed little threat. Luxottica continued to focus on large retailers, brand acquisitions, and licensing deals that fueled decades of growth. The status quo business model, which looked so good in the rearview mirror, had to be the answer when it came to looking forward through the windshield. Consumers had something to say about this and, while Warby Parker grew its physical store presence and increased its market share, Luxottica found itself in the unenviable role of playing catch-up.

Warby Parker was one of the pure digital retail concepts that successfully made the shift from online to physical. It experienced the ICSC's so-called "halo effect" of increasing online business in markets where it had a physical presence.

Consumers demand agency in how and where they spend their hard-earned money. They want the ability to meet a retail brand on their own terms. By opening a fleet of physical stores, Warby Parker allowed consumers to engage with the brand via its digital *and* physical sites.

What motivates employees and consumers?

In his book *Drive: The Surprising Truth About What Motivates Us*, Daniel Pink challenges the traditional view that rewards and punishments are effective motivators. While most leaders mistakenly impel their employees through extrinsic rewards and punishments, Pink argues that human motivation is largely intrinsic. Rather than using the outdated "carrot and stick" approach, which leads to dysfunction, Pink believes leaders should offer employees three intrinsic motivations:

Autonomy

People desire autonomy over task, time, techniques, and team. Giving people flexibility and choice leads to higher performance and satisfaction in the work world. The same is true of retailers. Winning retailers offer choice and flexibility in terms of channels, selection, and lifestyle (think Lululemon). Lululemon provides a seamless omnichannel shopping experience across physical stores, e-commerce, a branded app, and WeChat. It offers a wide assortment of products for women and men, with an ever-growing number of styles, colors, and categories, including self-care items, bags, and shoes. Lululemon also hosts in-store yoga and workshops, partners with studios and trainers for sponsored events, and focuses on empowerment through physical activity and mind-body connection. It is more of a movement than a retailer.

Mastery

Individuals will strive to continually improve at something that matters to them. Supporting mastery means allowing people to set achievable goals, get better at things step-by-step, and engage their interests. Likewise, retail has gone from general to specific; from department stores carrying everything, to specialty retailers catering to highly focused needs, like Warby Parker, Peloton, and Sur La Table.

Purpose

We want our work to contribute value and service to a cause larger and more enduring than ourselves. Tapping into meaning and purpose drives the highest levels of emotion. Many employees don't just work for paychecks; they work for purpose. And purpose is personified in leaders, more so than managers. People who work for paychecks can be measured by productivity (like in the industrial era). In the conceptual age and keyboard economy, those who work for purpose can be measured by effectiveness. How have employee actions and outcomes contributed to the greater good? Are the behaviors aligned with the company's strategic initiatives and the overarching company purpose?

Understanding the hybrid appeal (and making it work)

Key to the hybrid model is understanding human motivation. There have been many misperceptions about hybrid work. Many view the practice as an existential threat to the culture and collaboration of a business.

At its core, the hybrid model is driven by a renewed understanding of worker needs and aspirations. Key aspects of that consumer approach involve flexibility, autonomy, and optionality. Hybrid work is a combination of traditional forms of office work, along with an ecosystem of places for people to focus and work effectively. Remember, "office" and "work" are now separate from each other. "Work", as mentioned earlier, is a verb instead of a noun and therefore something people do, irrespective of place.

Here are some aspects of the hybrid model that people may find appealing:

Flexibility: The modern worker values the ability to balance personal and professional commitments without being tethered to a desk from nine to five. The hybrid model offers this flexibility, allowing for improved work-life balance. In fact, the employee as consumer is actually looking for life-work balance in the post-pandemic era, as we touched on in the previous chapter.

Collaboration and autonomy: While remote work provides autonomy, there's an undeniable magic in face-to-face interactions—the spontaneous brainstorming sessions, the coffee break chats, the team lunches. The hybrid model seeks to preserve this while also giving employees the freedom to choose where they work best.

So, what are some potential solutions and strategies that could enhance the hybrid model?

Dynamic workspace design: Traditional fixed-desk and cubicle layouts are giving way to more dynamic designs. Modular furniture, collaborative spaces, and reservable desks could become the norm. Resimercial (a combination of "residential" and "commercial") furniture has emerged where there was once only cubicles.

Here are some examples of resimercial designs from Walgreens' Technology Center of Excellence in Chicago's redeveloped Old Post Office.

Figure 9: Examples of Resimercial from Walgreens' Technology Center of Excellence in the Old Post Office, Chicago

Source: Stantec (www.stantec.com)

Source: Stantec (www.stantec.com)

Choice architecture: We introduced choice architecture in Chapter 5. Hybrid work requires the integration of classical and choice architecture, the blend between physical and behavioral constraints and opportunities. At its core, choice architecture is about empowering employees through subtle environmental cues rather than mandates. Some examples include:

- **Default options:** Carefully choosing default settings around things like meetings, schedules, workspace reservations, and communication preferences can subtly encourage productive behavior. These things need to be curated.

- **Simplify complex choices:** With hybrid work comes increased complexity in coordinating teams. Reducing complexity and driving clarity in company, team, and individual purpose and contribution leads to effective outcomes, rather than general productivity.

- **Autonomy and customization:** Allowing employees to personalize remote setups and routines respects individual needs, leading to higher satisfaction. The key is to align around effectiveness. Are employees contributing to the outcomes needed to move the enterprise forward? Hybrid work is a privilege, not a right.

Onboarding: Many companies are terrible at onboarding, which can have disastrous effects. Failure to effectively onboard from day one impacts employee retention, and can sour the attitudes and ambitions of otherwise enthusiastic newbies. Maybe the term "onboarding" is too clinical and sanitized. Clearly, companies want to curate a great first experience, which will lead to subsequent great experiences.

I read about a Toronto-based company called Klick Health, where each new hire starts on a Friday and therefore gets the weekend to decompress. Their first day starts with a meeting with the CEO who walks them through the company values. Then, in the afternoon, the new hire gets the honor of pushing an ice-cream cart around the office (the company's Friday tradition). The new hire is able to meet coworkers and engage with them in a fun, low-pressure setting. After all, who doesn't like ice cream?!

Tech integration: In workplaces where hot desking is the norm, advanced booking systems could allow employees to reserve desks on days they choose to come in. IoT devices could help in efficient energy management, ensuring areas not in use don't consume resources unnecessarily.

Community spaces: Parts of office buildings could transform into community spaces—areas for learning, collaboration, or even relaxation. Think in-house coffee shops, seminar areas, or wellness zones.

Salesforce is a leader in providing community spaces. The Ohana Floor (generally the top floor) can be reserved by employee groups or community groups. The space provides an amazing venue for participants.

Figure 10: Salesforce Tower, Ohana Floor, San Francisco

Source: Salesforce

New metrics: We are seeing a movement from KPIs (key performance indicators), a productivity construct, to OKRs (objectives and key results). OKRs help align teams and motivate people, and they make achieving the objective measurable. OKRs should be SMART: specific, measurable, attainable, relevant, and time-bound.

CASE STUDY
ATLASSIAN

When studying change and innovation, it's often beneficial to study extremes. Atlassian an Australian software company that makes team collaboration and productivity tools like Jira, Confluence, and Trello. Cofounder and co-CEO Scott Farquhar has been a strong proponent of flexible work arrangements for Atlassian's over 6,000 employees. The company also traditionally used KPIS to track progress and set goals. However, over time, it found KPIS led to local optimization, lack of alignment, and a focus on metrics over outcomes.

Atlassian transitioned to OKRS almost ten years ago. It saw OKRS as a way to get more clarity on priorities and coordination across global teams. In order to execute the migration, it started from the top. Executives worked with directors to cascade company objectives down and ensure team objectives contributed to higher level goals. Teams attended OKR training to learn the new framework. The program went live and each quarter thereafter, the company publicly tracked progress.

The results included increased transparency and strategic clarity across the organization, and better workflow between engineering, sales, and other functions to achieve shared goals. The company also saw higher employee satisfaction from purposeful and coherent goal setting and execution. Finally, the company saw sustained double-digit revenue growth demonstrating objectives were driving key outcomes.

Leveraging OKRS and focusing on outcomes allowed Atlassian to engage workers with flexible policies like "work anywhere," even before the pandemic. Moving forward, Atlassian is designing office locations with a focus on collaboration, not cubicles. Meeting spaces, cafes, and social areas are being built to encourage spontaneous in-person interactions. The company also encourages asynchronous communication and workflow, leveraged by its own products. In other words, it practices what it preaches. Farquhar also thinks hybrid work and thoughtful design (more on this in Chapter 8) are key elements for talent attraction and retention going forward.

CHAPTER SUMMARY

The rapid transition to hybrid work post-pandemic has significant implications for commercial real estate. As employees demand more flexibility, fixed cubicle layouts and rigid space allocation are giving way to dynamic designs with modular furniture and bookable areas. Building owners must revamp spaces to facilitate options for both focus and collaboration optimization. Leading companies are piloting advanced reservation systems, IoT integrations, and amenity reprograming to empower autonomous yet aligned remote/office workflows. These innovations will attract tenants seeking hybrid models supporting varied schedules and outcomes-driven culture.

As occupiers adjust goals and metrics to prioritize autonomy, mastery, and purpose over mere productivity, real estate partners must understand shifting motivations. Choice architecture, evolving default settings and simplified spaces, can subtly boost optimal behaviors for health, learning, and interactions. Onboardings also require reconfiguration to engage newcomers amid a now hybrid-native generation entering the workforce. Creative short-term space agreements may seed long-term commitments for agile organizations.

It's important to remember that ribbon cuttings are the beginning, not the end. The real, curated work starts when the space opens and the employees use the space the way they want. It's leadership's responsibility to observe behavior and course correct for an optimal employee experience, which will ultimately lead to optimal business outcomes.

8

SUSTAINABLE AND SMART DESIGN

*"Design is not just what it looks like
and feels like. Design is how it works."*

STEVE JOBS

AMID THE DISCOURSE on the future of work and real estate, there's an undercurrent that cannot be ignored: sustainability. The global clarion call for eco-conscious living and working isn't just a trend; it's a necessity. In the sphere of office real estate, sustainability isn't just about "going green"—it's about creating spaces that are future-ready, resilient, and responsible. It's about enabling agility, the ability to move quickly and easily.

Furthermore, today's working population is more attuned to a company's overriding social responsibility approach and fundamental meaning as a business. Having purpose involves being a good global corporate citizen. Whether the company develops and owns or occupies real estate, employees and consumers of the built environment are focusing on sustainability. It's no longer a nice-to-have and, in some instances, it is a competitive advantage.

In this chapter, we discuss the importance of "healthy" and smart buildings, and consider some of the green practices becoming increasingly common in modern workspaces. We then shift our focus to design and architecture, looking at the retail success of Apple, and what the office real estate sector can learn from this with regard to thoughtful and intentional design.

Healthy and smart buildings

On a macro level, buildings are the largest contributor to global warming and the real estate sector accounts for thirty-eight per cent of all greenhouse gas emissions. Buildings emit more greenhouse gas emissions than electricity production, shipping, and aviation combined. On a personal level, particularly in the post-pandemic era, more and more people are concerned about indoor air quality (IAQ) and "healthy" buildings.

Before the pandemic, IAQ was not a top priority for building owners and managers. HVAC systems were often focused on temperature and comfort, not necessarily bringing in fresh outside air. In most buildings, the windows are sealed so the only alternative for additional fresh air is from the HVAC system.

The pandemic highlighted the importance of ventilation and air exchange, diluting and removing virus particles from indoor spaces. Poorly ventilated indoor environments were linked to a higher risk of spread. While most focused on hand sanitizer and sanitizing wipes, few focused on the real culprit—air quality.

Minimum codes specify a minimum fresh air intake of approximately one to two air changes per hour (ACH). By comparison, most residential systems are designed for 0.35

to one ACH. Modern HVAC buildings are generally designed for three to six ACH while older buildings continue to run at one to two ACH. The Centers for Disease Control and Prevention (CDC) recommends at least five ACH along with filtration rated according to the Minimum Efficiency Reporting Value (MERV) of thirteen.

Most employees don't know about ACH or MERV. However, owners, managers, and occupiers responsible for making decisions on office space need to understand the importance of choosing "healthier" buildings.

The key question to ask is: is your building smart?

The convergence of technology and sustainability has given birth to the concept of "smart buildings." These structures leverage IoT devices, AI, and data analytics to optimize energy use, enhance security, and improve occupant comfort. They adjust heating based on occupancy, manage lighting based on natural sunlight, and even monitor air quality in real time.

Beyond individual buildings, the broader vision is for "smart cities"—urban environments where everything from traffic management to waste disposal is optimized using technology, all with sustainability at the core.

Green practices in modern workspaces

Here are some of the ways in which modern workspaces are going green—and the benefits gained as a result.

Energy efficiency

The incorporation of energy-efficient appliances, optimized lighting solutions, and advanced HVAC systems can significantly reduce a building's carbon footprint. Incorporating energy-efficient systems and appliances significantly lowers utility costs for businesses. With savings generated, companies can invest in other priorities that improve the workplace. Employees benefit from a more stable cost structure as well. Efficient lighting also enhances visual comfort and productivity for knowledge workers. Advanced HVAC systems ensure precise temperature and airflow for occupant health. By maximizing comfort year round, worker satisfaction and performance increases.

Green building materials

Sustainable building materials like recycled steel emit far fewer harmful chemicals and are better for indoor air quality than conventional alternatives. This enhances the health and wellbeing of employees who spend most of their days inside. Green materials also have superior acoustical properties that minimize distracting noise levels. Combined with their increased durability, sustainable options lead to longer intervals between renovations and improvements. This means fewer disruptions and more stable work environments over the long run.

Waste management

Robust recycling, composting, and waste reduction programs implemented in offices make workers feel good about their company's environmental commitment. It fosters employee pride in the workplace. Streamlined sorting and collection bins make it very convenient for building occupants to participate in waste management efforts on a daily basis. This improves recycling participation rates over traditional trash-only collection. Strong waste diversion efforts also convey that resource efficiency extends beyond just energy to entire facility operations. In some ways, obvious recycling receptacles and written reminders reinforce the enterprise's commitment to sustainability. Moving from nice-to-have to must-have, the absence of a program will draw more attention than the presence of a program, even if it's minimal.

Indoor environmental quality

Beyond just the external environment, sustainable offices also prioritize the internal environment. This means ensuring ample natural light, good air quality (as discussed earlier), and green spaces that can enhance employee wellbeing.

Design

Proper physical architecture and choice architecture intersect at design. Modern design seeks to deploy natural materials, like wood, with flexible materials and installations, allowing for maximum agility. Rolling furniture, demountable fixtures, magnetic surfaces, and reconfigurable ceiling systems all contribute to space agility.

Offices are moving away from fixed to movable walls, taking another page from the hotel industry's book. Multiple vignettes allow workers to vote with their feet regarding where they collaborate and where they focus individually. As mentioned in the XY Sense case study in Chapter 4, companies can observe workers' behavior and change out vignettes that aren't used, replacing them with more popular designs. Movable walls provide the agility without the landfill burden of more rigid designs. Changing hard walls involves permitting and demolition. Movable walls bypass the need for demolition and therefore landfill.

CASE STUDY
THE EDGE

Often dubbed the "greenest office building in the world," The Edge in Amsterdam sets a benchmark in sustainable design. In fact, it has the highest sustainability rating for an office building. It generates more electricity than it consumes through solar panels, wind turbines, and geothermal energy. This saves over 1.2 million kilowatt-hours (kWh) annually. The building harvests rainwater for restroom facilities, and deploys 28,000 sensors to monitor light, temperature, air quality, and more to optimize energy based on occupancy and daylight. In fact, the building provides ultra-fresh air supply that is 500 per cent more fresh than code.

Materials are made from sustainably harvested timber, as well as recycled materials, and finished without volatile organic compounds (which have a high vapor pressure and low water solubility). Natural light and views are provided for ninety per cent of workspaces.

What does this all mean to the building owner and the corporate occupiers? For the building owner, occupancy rates have been over ninety-eight per cent since 2015. Rents have remained fairly stable pre- and post-pandemic, commanding 270 to 320 euros per square meter.

In 2022, the building was valued at 500 million euros, up from 450 million euros in 2019 (before the pandemic). The upfront capital investments in sustainability yield significant long-term savings through drastically reduced utility and maintenance costs, creating a competitive differentiator versus other buildings in the market. No major tenants left due to the pandemic. In fact, companies like Microsoft and Deloitte are attracted to the building's wellness features, important to hybrid work.

For corporate occupiers and employees, the level of sustainability significantly impacts recruitment and retention. Companies want to be located in buildings demonstrating environmental leadership. Workers are attracted to the wellness benefits, including amenities like gyms, restaurants, and lockers, with plenty of green space and biophilia. The robust infrastructure of The Edge supports hybrid work by connecting consumers to work, amenities, nature, and wellness, creating a relevant, desirable, and successful environment for all.

The Apple look

In the area of design and architecture, the FoW will, once again, benefit from lessons learned from the retail industry. The greatest example of retail design and architecture driving consumer adoption is Apple.

Have you ever read the entire user's manual for an iPhone? No? Of course not—because the design is so intuitive you don't need one. Steve Jobs and Jony Ive, Apple's former senior vice president of industrial design and chief design officer, manically focused on a distinctive, minimalist design aesthetic that places a strong emphasis on simplicity, functionality, and sleek modernity across all Apple products and retail spaces.

The Simon Sinek "why" discussion earlier in the book provides a great delineation between Apple and Dell. They both offer technology derived from readily available components, yet Apple tells you to "think different" while Dell is simply trying to sell units. Design and approach matter.

Some features of Apple's design aesthetic include:

- **Clean lines and minimalism:** Apple products feature clean, simple, geometric lines and shapes without decorative flourishes or visual clutter. The emphasis is on the product and interface itself; Apple removes anything that distracts from core utility.

- **White and light:** Open white spaces and light create a sense of spacious modernity across Apple stores and product packaging. This projects approachability.

- **Glass and metal:** Sleek materials like glass, aluminum, and stainless steel convey high-tech quality through iconic devices like the iPhone and MacBook. Reflective surfaces add depth.

- **Touch centric:** Apple shifted electronics from buttons to seamless touch-based interactions using hand gestures, taps, and swipes for intuitive control.

- **Asymmetry:** Many Apple products feature asymmetrical lines that convey modernity while improving ergonomics for functionality like camera usage.

- **Enduring foundations:** Apple's core DNA around simplicity, modernity, and a seamless user experience has persisted at the tech giant across decades.

This "Apple look" provides a timeless, reductionist aesthetic tailored to placing content, tasks, and user needs at the forefront through well-defined visual order and intuitive interaction.

That design helped revolutionize Apple's retail experience, too. So much so that malls often report sales per square foot with and without Apple's contribution. Great design makes sense and cents. In 2022, the average Apple Store produced sales over 8,000 dollars per square foot per year. In comparison, fast fashion retailers, like H&M, deliver around 2,000 dollars per square foot per year while the typical mall retailer averages under 300 dollars per square foot per year. For further context, high-end luxury retailers like Louis Vuitton and Tiffany & Co. deliver around 3,000 dollars and 2,900 dollars respectively per square foot. No other brand draws more value from smaller physical footprints than Apple based on sales-per-square-foot metrics.

What are the keys to that design? The process started in the early 2000s when Steve Jobs approached Sir Norman Foster to help design the early Apple stores. Foster + Partners translated Steve Jobs' vision into physical form, resulting in signature Apple Store features including the all-glass box entrance, providing transparency and continuity from outside to inside. In addition to the physical design, Apple incorporated choice architecture, heightening the overall experience. Key innovations include roaming associates, expertly trained and knowledgeable, the Genius Bar, creative workspaces, and an open and operating environment to explore all available technology. Free year-round workshops on photography, art, design, and so on drive continuous engagement between consumers and brand.

We have already explored the ways in which work is changing. Undoubtedly, the consumer, or employee, is king. So, what changes need to happen to support the agility required for the future of work? Key themes, highlighted by Apple, include: variety of spaces, encouragement of exploration, creative workspaces, and a focus on experiences. Leasing 20,000 square feet and filling the office with cubicles won't cut it in the conceptual age. The keyboard economy deserves, and demands, better design.

Drawing inspiration from Apple's signature retail design and aesthetic, which continues to successfully engage customers worldwide, here are ten key attributes for future workplaces to similarly engage and inspire employees (and boost effectiveness):

1. **Open transparency:** Eliminate physical and metaphorical barriers with glass or other transparent architecture, remote working capabilities, and free flows of communication.

2. **Clean sophistication:** Convey excellence and quality through non-distracting, minimalist environments using well-chosen accents.

3. **Natural light:** Create well-lit spaces with atriums, light wells, and mimicked outdoor light promoting energy, focus, and cheer.

4. **Communal hubs:** Develop central spaces for congregation, collaboration, and hosting visitors to drive a sense of community.

5. **Flexible spaces:** Support needs for different settings with lounge spaces, private enclaves, standing desks, and adaptable configurations.

6. **Integrated technology:** Make capabilities available in the background for when you need them with intuitive voice- and touch-based controls.

7. **Focus on wellness:** Make movement, nutrition, and recharging simple through onsite gyms, healthy snack offerings, nap pods, and more.

8. **Sustainability:** As discussed earlier in the chapter, maintain commitment to sustainability through the use of responsible materials, renewable energy, smart sensors, and conservation efforts.

9. **Accessibility:** Ensure all workers can navigate spaces seamlessly regardless of age, language or ability through inclusive, barrier-free design.

10 **Cultural inspiration:** Infuse spaces with authentic signals of an organization's values, purpose, and passion. For Apple, both office and retail locations are characterized by simplicity and minimalism. Open spaces over closed offices encourage collaboration. The circular design of Apple Park's (Apple's HQ) main building is meant to drive innovation and creativity.

By making the workplace inspire people like Apple stores inspire customers, companies can drive engagement, boost satisfaction, and better identify with their workforce to power the future of work.

CASE STUDY
JPMORGAN CHASE

When Jamie Dimon decided to create a new headquarters building for JPMC at 270 Park Avenue in New York City, he took a page out of Steve Jobs' book and turned to Foster + Partners and its founder, Norman Foster. This building represents the perfect fusion of consumer primacy, building on the successes of Apple in retail with a whole new future of work.

The building is described by Foster + Partners as follows: "The 1,388-foot, 60-story skyscraper will be New York City's largest all-electric tower with net zero operational emissions and exceptional indoor air quality that exceeds the highest standards in sustainability, health and wellness. It will help define the modern workplace with 21st century infrastructure, smart technology and 2.5 million square feet of flexible and collaborative space that can easily adapt to the future of work.

"The new building will house up to 14,000 employees—replacing an outdated facility designed in the late 1950s for about 3,500 employees. It will offer 2.5 times more outdoor space on the ground level of Park and Madison Avenues, featuring wider sidewalks and a large public plaza on Madison Avenue with natural green space and other amenities ... [The building] will be 100 per cent powered by renewable energy sourced from a New York State hydroelectric plant ... The project also recycled, reused or upcycled 97% of the building materials from the demolition—far exceeding the 75% requirement of the leading green building standard."

270 Park Avenue encapsulates both architectural design and choice architecture, along with sustainable design and practices. While Dimon is famously in the RTO (return to office) camp, he understands, better than most, the potential for urban doom loops to develop in central business districts. One thing is for sure: 270 Park Avenue will be one of the premiere office buildings in Manhattan. Employees will want to spend time in the building with colleagues and clients.

CHAPTER SUMMARY

Sustainability is becoming an imperative in the real estate sector. As the largest contributor to global greenhouse gas emissions, buildings must transition to reduce their environmental impact. The pandemic highlighted the importance of indoor air quality and well-ventilated buildings.

Green building techniques—like energy-efficient systems, sustainable materials, and robust recycling programs—offer multiple benefits. They provide cost savings through reduced utility bills and less maintenance. Healthier indoor environments boost occupant wellbeing, satisfaction, and productivity. Sustainable practices also aid in tenant recruitment and retention. Exemplars like The Edge in Amsterdam demonstrate these advantages, commanding premium rents with near-full occupancy despite the challenges of the pandemic.

The convergence of sustainability and technology is giving rise to smart, data-driven buildings and cities. IoT sensors, analytics, and control systems optimize performance factors from energy use to security. Flexible, adaptable designs allow structures to reuse and repurpose spaces over decades of change. As net zero carbon goals loom, the built environment must harness renewable technology and prioritize embodied carbon reductions.

There are other design considerations, too. This chapter discussed how intentional design and architecture can help support the future of work. It looked at lessons that can be learned from Apple's renowned retail design under Steve Jobs. This intuitive design has helped drive strong sales performance in Apple stores, demonstrating how great design can resonate strongly with consumers and improve business metrics.

To incorporate these retail lessons into the workplace, the chapter advocated for design principles like transparency, natural light, varied workspaces, integrated technology, accessibility, and sustainability. Communal hubs and flexible configurations that support different activities were also emphasized. Drawing inspiration from prominent brands like Apple can help attract top talent.

The new JPMorgan CHASE headquarters was highlighted as an example that incorporates many of these ideas through its sustainable design, collaborative floorplans, and goal of defining the future work experience. For organizations to thrive amid rapid change, intentional architecture with employees in mind will remain important for engagement, productivity, and adapting to evolving needs.

9

LEADERSHIP IN THE FUTURE OF WORK

"When you replace hierarchy and top-down decision making with trust and shared understanding, people are empowered together to pursue what really matters most."

L. DAVID MARQUET

IN A WORLD where the very fabric of "work" is undergoing transformation, the role of leadership is more critical than ever. With seismic shifts in workplace dynamics, real estate configurations, and technological integrations, leaders face the arduous task of navigating uncharted territories.

Technology is changing faster than ever. Consumer behavior is following suit. We see Schumpeter's "creative destruction" in all aspects of life. In order to survive and thrive in today's world, successful change management is fundamental. Without modern leadership, change management initiatives are doomed to fail. In fact, according to research conducted by McKinsey & Company, upwards of seventy per cent of organizational and structural changes fail due to poor change management.

Leading through today's challenges is getting increasingly hard. Course-correcting and changing one's business is exceedingly more difficult, particularly for businesses that have enjoyed the benefits of maintaining the status quo for decades. Old department store operators like Sears, Montgomery Ward, Gimbels, and Sterns all had a good thing going, until they didn't.

How have retail leaders adapted to consumer primacy, and what can businesses and building owners learn around leadership in the face of accelerating technology and consumer behavior change? This chapter delves into the evolving role of leadership against the backdrop of these profound changes.

Leading Walmart into the 21st century

In 1980, Walmart was the third largest retailer (by revenue) in the United States behind Sears and Kmart. Walmart became the biggest retailer in the world in 1991, fueled by rural growth, supply chain innovation, buying power and scale, and one-stop shopping in Walmart Supercenters. The company responded to consumer demand better than any other retailer at scale.

Amazon launched as an online bookseller in 1995. Amazon wasn't even on Walmart's radar as a competitor, but the notion that consumers would buy online was gaining traction, so Walmart launched its first e-commerce site in 1998. Then in 2007, Walmart acquired a minor stake in Chinese online marketplace JD.com to tap into the emerging e-commerce market in China. Apple released the first iPhone the same year. The advent of the iPhone, along with emerging e-commerce options, marked a key milestone for consumer primacy.

Meanwhile, following an ill-fated merger between Sears and Kmart that doomed both brands into obscurity, the e-commerce footrace between Walmart and Amazon was heating up. We started hearing "last mile" in the common lexicon. The last mile in retail refers to the last leg of the delivery journey that brings an order from a distribution hub to the consumer's doorstep. It is considered one of the most expensive and challenging parts of the fulfillment process due to inefficiencies like low vehicle utilization and inability to consolidate deliveries. But once it arrived, it was here to stay. Consumers liked getting what they wanted, when they wanted—and they wanted more, faster.

Amazon acquired Whole Foods in 2017 for 13.7 billion dollars, creating a direct afront to Walmart's grocery business. The Amazon acquisition was a wake-up call for grocery chains, Walmart included. Creative strategies encouraging consumers to "buy online and pick up in-store" began to proliferate. Consumers could shop the aisles, order online and have their shopping bags placed directly in the trunk of their car, or order online and have the groceries delivered directly to their doorstep. From 1998 to 2023, Walmart notched a stock increase in market value of over 292 billion dollars while Amazon saw its market cap top one trillion dollars during that same time.

In response to the Whole Foods acquisition by Amazon, Walmart worked to bolster its own fresh food offerings, expanded grocery pickup and delivery options, cut prices on some Whole Foods products, and started allowing returns of Amazon purchases to its stores. Technology truly impacted the grocery business and the consumer benefited with more choice, accessibility, and pricing power.

Just as Amazon chief Jeff Bezos engineered the e-commerce revolution, Doug McMillon, and Mike Duke before him, led Walmart into the twenty-first century, accelerating online offerings atop Walmart's already industry-leading physical footprint.

Doug McMillon is most credited with steering the Walmart ship and adapting to the rise of e-commerce. Key to that adaptation were the following points:

- **Omnichannel strategies:** As we've discussed in previous chapters, this includes offering the consumer choice and respecting their agency to decide where, when, and how they want to shop.

- **Consumer data:** As consumers engaged across multiple channels, the smart retailers (with Walmart and Amazon at the top of the list) tracked web traffic, online purchases, changes in buying behavior, and meta-data associated with search in order to improve and customize the retail offering. Whole new teams of data analytics and business intelligence emerged to support these efforts.

- **Logistics and supply chain networks:** Retailers needed to develop sophisticated and complex supply chain networks to accommodate omnichannel fulfillment and returns. Technology included more advanced inventory management systems and predictive analytics to ensure product was in the right place at the right time.

- **Technology and innovation:** Certain technology created seamless and intuitive digital experiences for consumers. Consumers had the power in their hands, literally. Specific apps allowed for shopping and ordering. Consumers could fill their "basket" throughout the day and "check out" when it suited them. They could decide if the product was to be delivered or picked up. For pickup, technology evolved to alert in-store personnel upon your arrival via the app. This was especially prescient during the pandemic as groceries were placed in car trunks so as to minimize human interaction.

McMillon and Walmart were able to adapt and evolve priorities to compete for—and claim—their share of the consumer's wallet.

Irrespective of industry, the future of work depends on leaders adapting and evolving—just as Doug McMillon did. This is where it's important to note, once again, that leadership is different from management. Far too many corporates focus on management over leadership when it should be the other way around.

Leadership > management

As I've stated several times throughout this book, one of the biggest fallacies of the pre-pandemic work era was productivity—a vestige from the industrial era when factories turned inputs into outputs using machines with human intervention. Output per hour, defect rates, and utilization rates were common. Managers monitored workers. The world of management was hierarchical and top-down. Managers focused on direct oversight and controlling operations in a centralized workplace.

Some of the loudest voices and most fervent advocates for RTO are the middle managers, who only know how to manage via the "butts in seats" approach. If staff are in their assigned stations, they must be working and being productive. We all know the flawed nature of this thinking.

In his fantastic book, *Turn the Ship Around!*, David Marquet tells his story of commanding the USS *Santa Fe* in 1999. The *Santa Fe* was known for having poor morale and performance. Marquet introduced a revolutionary new leadership approach of "giving control" rather than "taking control." He focused on building leadership capabilities in his crew and pushing decision-making authority down to lower levels.

Captain Marquet's book highlights the progressive leadership needed to succeed and excel in the conceptual age and the era of hybrid work. The FoW is focused on outcomes. Marquet asked questions rather than giving direct orders. He empowered his crew to take initiative and own solutions. He moved from a command-and-control structure to mission command where execution is decentralized, leaders provide "intent" or desired outcomes, trust is a two-way street, and risk—and even failure—is tolerated for the benefit of improving outcomes.

Here are some of the key lessons from Marquet's book about transforming culture via leadership rather than management:

- **Empower your people:** Give them ownership and authority to make decisions. Don't micromanage. Let them learn through responsibility.

- **Replace top-down control with leadership:** Model the desired behaviors. Coach and mentor. Ask questions rather than give orders.

- **Unlock intrinsic motivation:** Connect work to larger meaning and purpose. Enable mastery, autonomy, and progress. Satisfy people's need to contribute.

- **Flatten hierarchies:** Remove unnecessary layers of bureaucracy. Communicate directly across ranks. Listen to input from all levels.

- **Encourage disciplined initiative:** Set clear goals and constraints. Give people freedom to determine how to achieve goals. Hold them accountable. Reward those who demonstrate initiative.

- **Implement small changes systematically:** Don't try to change everything at once. Introduce changes in a logical sequence. Evaluate and improve.

- **Actively practice and develop leadership:** Treat leadership as a capability to cultivate, not an innate characteristic. Invest in developing leadership skills at all levels.

- **Persist through resistance:** Expect pushback against cultural change. Listen to concerns but stay firm on the vision and goals.

- **Remember that success breeds success:** Let small wins gain momentum. Celebrate and publicize successes. Build on each advance.

- **Focus on instilling ownership and aligning purpose:** Empower your people and lead through clarity, communication, and coaching, not control.

FoW leaders would do well to adopt the mission focus over command and control. The conceptual age calls for agility, critical thinking, and enhanced decision-making ability—all of which drive toward clearly articulated outcomes. Those outcomes are generally focused on improving customer experience (CX), developing new innovations and IP, extending market reach in a globalized economy, and using enhanced technology to improve speed, efficiency, and cost for established work.

Leaders make the future

In 2012, futurist Bob Johansen published his book, *Leaders Make the Future*. The message, along with his forecast at the time, remains prescient. He posits that the world is influenced by four factors: volatility, uncertainty, complexity, and ambiguity, or VUCA. In addition, the future portends four important changes:

1 The world will become even more complex;

2 Leaders will face both "danger and opportunity;"

3 Leaders will need non-traditional skills to shape the future; and

4 Traditional approaches will no longer suffice to meet the challenges ahead.

Johansen advocates for flipping VUCA to move from:

- volatility   to vision
- uncertainty   to understanding
- complexity   to clarity
- ambiguity   to agility

To do so, he outlines ten cutting-edge leadership skills. For the purposes of consumer primacy and the FoW, we will focus on three of them: clarity, rapid prototyping, and commons creating.

Clarity

The VUCA world will leave many people confused. They will expect their leaders to see through "messes and contradictions" and to provide real solutions. Clarity is different from "certainty," which is more restrictive and rules-oriented. The best leaders digest input from others, discern and communicate the best path without providing "false hope," and embrace uncertainty as they determine their way forward. Most important of all: ensuring leaders are clear about the purpose of the enterprise. As I stated previously, many

employees work for specific leaders and/or a sense of purpose, not just paychecks.

Rapid prototyping

As we previously discussed, the ribbon cutting for a new office
is the beginning, not the end. Rapid prototyping is a hallmark
of design thinking. Fail fast. Try things and break things. We
see that the most successful new work designs involve flexibility and agility. Hard walls are passe. The office sector is
taking inspiration from the hotel industry with movable walls
and a myriad of vignettes for sitting, gathering, solo work,
and collaboration. The acceleration of technology is putting
pressure on leaders to plan and figure out the answers instead
of "learn as you go" while observing the behavior of key con-
stituents: the employees. Rapid prototyping accepts failure
as critical to success.

Commons creating

Traditional commons are geographic spaces devoted to public
benefit, like parks, town squares, beaches, and markets. In
the conceptual age, creating common ground broadens the
basics and elevates the requirement to build an ecosystem of
physical and digital spaces that offer choice and autonomy
for individuals to excel and companies to prosper. Companies will need to move beyond the notion of WFH or remote
work and adapt to the holistic approach of hybrid work, as
outlined in Chapter 7. To fuel hybrid work, the ecosystem of
places needs to be hub-like, supported by spokes or satellite
locations. Those spokes can be directly owned or leased, or
flexible office space. Technology needs to be the common
thread connecting the commons across the ecosystems.
Proper commons creating will allow consumers/employ-
ees to vote with their feet regarding when, where, and how
they work.

The pillars of conceptual age leadership

Leadership is a learned art. It continues to evolve along with technology and consumer behavior. The industries that will fuel the twenty-first century will involve data and new technology. These companies will scale faster than the manufacturing companies that dominated the twentieth century, and therefore the workspace will need to evolve and adapt at pace. Leadership, more than management, will need to ensure employees have the vision, purpose, and understanding to be truly effective for their enterprise. There are eight pillars of conceptual age leadership:

1. **Adaptability:** Gone are the days when strategies were etched in stone. Today's leaders need the agility to pivot, embracing change as the only constant.

2. **Digital literacy:** A basic understanding of technology is no longer sufficient. Leaders must be conversant with the latest digital tools, platforms, and trends that shape their industries.

3. **Emotional intelligence (EQ):** As work environments become more flexible and diverse, leaders must exhibit high EQ—understanding, empathizing with, and connecting with team members from varied backgrounds and with different perspectives.

4. **Building trust:** In virtual or hybrid setups, where face-to-face interactions are limited, establishing trust becomes paramount. This requires transparent communication, consistency in actions, and a culture of mutual respect.

5. **Overcoming "out of sight, out of mind":** Leaders must ensure that remote team members feel included and valued. Regular check-ins, virtual team-building exercises, and inclusive communication can help bridge the gap.

6 **Measuring effectiveness:** The shift from "hours clocked" to "tasks accomplished" requires a rethinking of performance metrics. Leaders must champion outcome-based evaluations over traditional time-based assessments.

7 **Ethical considerations:** As AI and automation integrate deeper into operations, leaders will grapple with ethical dilemmas. This includes fair employment practices, data privacy concerns, and ensuring technology augments human roles rather than diminishes them.

8 **Continuous learning:** The rapid pace of technological evolution means that learning can never cease. Leaders must champion a culture of continuous education, both for themselves and their teams.

CHAPTER SUMMARY

As you know, the retail sector has seen dramatic transformation driven by evolving consumer preferences and technology. Leaders at the helm of retailers like Walmart adapted by embracing omnichannel retail, leveraging data, revamping supply chains, and providing intuitive digital experiences. Meanwhile, retailers unable to adapt, like Sears, declined rapidly. This underscores how critical effective leadership is in times of great change.

The future of work calls for a new leadership approach focused more on empowerment than control. Rather than micromanaging, leaders must encourage ownership, align work to purpose, coach rather than command, and promote initiative within clear goals. Skills like emotional intelligence, communication, and change management become vital. Traditional metrics like productivity matter less than effectiveness. Yet many managers still cling to old assumptions about physical presence equating to productivity, damaging employee engagement and trust.

Navigating the landscape of hybrid work requires rethinking policies, spaces, and technology, rethinking consumer behavior and requirements, and emphasizing culture, innovation, and effectiveness. Leaders must provide clarity amid uncertainty, rapidly prototype solutions to challenges, and foster a common culture across distributed teams through transparent communication and empathy. Adaptability, digital literacy, and emotional intelligence are key pillars of conceptual age leadership. By putting people first, directing technology ethically, and championing continuous learning, leaders can activate potential despite complexity.

The core emphasis is on the heightened importance of more collaborative, coaching-based, and empowering leadership approaches in a climate of exponential technological and social change. Control-focused management is proving inadequate—leaders must instead tap into employees' intrinsic motivations (as outlined in Chapter 7) and help workers gain purpose from effectiveness.

CONCLUSION
WHERE TO NEXT?

"When written in Chinese, the word 'crisis'
is composed of two characters. One represents
danger, and the other represents opportunity."
JOHN F. KENNEDY

THE FUTURE OF work is the future of consumer behavior. Beyond that, it's near impossible to forecast large, impactful events. For the future of work, we have the benefit of near-recent shopping patterns. The good news is that the people shopping are generally the same people working. But prognostication is a messy business, best left to economists and meteorologists.

The Economist publishes a "year ahead" edition each January. In its January 2020 edition, there was no mention of the pandemic, nor was there any mention of Russia invading Ukraine in the January 2022 edition. That is not to take the editors of *The Economist* to task. It's just that events happen that are unpredicted—at least in terms of timing. Certainly, at the time of writing, the unwritten geopolitical, health, and macroeconomic forecasting is as cloudy as ever. Regardless of what "black swan" events may happen in the future, we know that technology will continue to accelerate at faster and faster rates.

We live in a VUCA world and, for the most part, things are getting more VUCA (volatile, uncertain, complex, and ambiguous). So, how do we approach multimillion-dollar decisions on commercial real estate when the world is changing faster and faster? What considerations are needed? What tools need to be deployed?

Many futurists opine that today is the slowest rate of change you will ever experience. I believe this and history proves this out. Understanding this baseline will allow businesses to better envision and prepare for the future.

In Morgan Housel's 2023 book, *Same as Ever: A Guide to What Never Changes,* he submits, "Predicting what the world will look like fifty years from now is impossible. But predicting that people will still respond to greed, fear, opportunity, exploitation, risk, uncertainty, tribal affiliations, and social persuasion in the same way is a bet I'd take." While the world around us is changing rapidly, people remain fundamentally the same.

The future of both work and retail real estate is deeply rooted in human behavior. To quote Tom Stat, "... at the root of change and the innovations that fuel them, are deeply rooted demand for mobility, our need to gather, our desire to interact, our pursuit of meaning and fulfillment, and our desire for mission and purpose." While there are no silver bullets concerning the future of real estate, we know the answers lie in observing human behavior and adapting accordingly.

The impact of accelerating technology

Chapter 1 outlined the history of technological platform shifts by looking in the rearview mirror. Chapter 3 offered a glimpse through the windshield concerning technological acceleration and expansion in areas like quantum computing and synthetic biology.

Advances in technology will continue to impact consumers. Those who spend money in retail and those who make money through work. We will continue to see consumer primacy trends involving agency, autonomy, and optionality.

Strategy, planning, innovation, execution, and learning must be consumer-centric for both retail and work. The retail industry has a twenty-year head start. Work and office will do well to learn from retailers' successes and failures (just a few of which are highlighted in this book).

The power of consumers is, therefore, the driving factor for both the future of retail and the future of work. Driven by accelerating technology, we see how consumer behavior is shaping and reshaping the world in which we live.

So, where is commercial real estate going? The office sector is as unfavorable as ever from an investor standpoint. In contrast, retail is resurging due to lack of supply and increasing demand, particularly for essential or daily needs businesses. The live/work/play, healthy ecosystem continues to support changing consumer behavior.

The office asset class will continue to be a slow-moving car crash for the next several years. Aging and functionally obsolete buildings will experience the same existential threat as class B and class C malls and retail locations over the past decade. There is indeed a Darwinian moment afoot. Some estimates suggest that the office asset class is valued at $1.8 trillion, a forty per cent decline from the pre-pandemic $3 trillion valuation.

So, what does the future hold?

Here are some educated forecasts about the future of work and office real estate:

The future of work

Work is evolving, which means workspaces will need to evolve and adapt as well. Third places will proliferate and corporate occupiers will need to rethink the network of places and the connectivity between those places.

Hybrid work models are here to stay

The pandemic has shown that many roles can effectively operate remotely. As a result, a combination of in-office and remote work, or the hybrid model, is likely to become the norm for numerous organizations. We saw in retail's evolution where omnichannel or e-commerce advanced on the back of accelerating technology. Hybrid work and omnichannel retail are two sides of the same coin. The common denominator is the employee or consumer.

There are many examples of remote-first companies—Atlassian, for instance. With employees spread across the globe, work is continuous across days and time zones. Projects are advanced by employees who hand off tasks to colleagues in different parts of the world.

Leadership is essential to ensure maximum productivity and/or effectiveness in a hybrid work model. Dilbert methods of "management by butts in seats" are quickly becoming anachronistic.

During the pandemic, crowdsourcing research led to some interesting observations. Namely, onsite activity becoming the new offsite meeting. Many thought they hated their job. It turns out they hated their commute. One of the most prescient thoughts was the overriding necessity for purposeful presence over passive attendance. Employees were calculating their return on commute and determining if it was worth traveling, in some instances, ninety minutes each way, simply to sit at their assigned stations and attend Zoom calls. Purposeful presence requires a relevant reason to attend the office in-person.

On a practical level, the hybrid work model will need to be curated by leadership. Building owners will need to provide relevant amenities, like quality food options, services, exercise facilities, and so on. The Old Post Office in Chicago was renovated to include a boxing gym on the mezzanine and paddle tennis courts on the three-acre roof. There is also an increased focus on indoor air quality, natural light, and supporting biophilia.

Growth and consolidation of flexible offices

In addition to traditional offices, a third type of place will continue to thrive and be more relevant. The flexible office industry continues to grow, despite the headlines about coworking company WeWork's bankruptcy filing. In fact, WeWork only accounts for 700 of the 30,000 global flexible offices—just 2.3 per cent market share. I expect to see significant growth and consolidation in the flexible office business. Particularly given that, of those 30,000 locations, the top player, IWG, has approximately 4,000 of them, or thirteen per cent market share.

Expansion of "third places"

The expansion of third places will continue to flourish. Hotels, airline lounges, universities, and even restaurants can all serve as hybrid work locations. As we've discussed, work is something you do, irrespective of location.

Fundamental to those third places are gatherings, interactions, and experiences of human beings being together.

Hybrid takes otherwise static places and makes them kinetic for ideas, engagement, and sharing.

So, who is doing hybrid the best right now?
Take a look at the following case studies...

- **Spotify**—Implemented a "work from anywhere" policy where employees can choose whether to work from home or the office. Focuses on employees meeting outcomes rather than having set hours or locations. Provides a coworking stipend for employees to use when working remotely.

- **Siemens**—Introduced a hybrid model where employees can work two to three days in the office and the rest remotely. Provides training and change management support around hybrid work. Emphasizes autonomy and trust in employees to get work done productively.

- **Dell**—Gives employees freedom to work where they want. Facilitates communication between distributed teams with digital tools. Trains managers to lead remote teams effectively. Measures performance based on results, not presence.

- **Salesforce**—Created a flexible "Success From Anywhere" model with two to three days in the office. Invested in cloud technology and collaboration tools. Focuses on employee wellbeing, and providing the space and tools for employees to thrive.

The keys for successful hybrid work tend to be flexibility, collaboration tools, manager training, and a results-focused culture. Companies on the cutting edge are rethinking their space needs and empowering employees to work productively regardless of location.

The future of office space
What are the key considerations around office space in the conceptual age? What should owners and occupiers be thinking about?

Increased use of flexible office spaces
With fluctuating numbers of employees in the office on any given day due to hybrid models, we may see a move toward more flexible, modular office setups. Spaces will be adaptable, able to serve as a meeting room one day and a collaborative workspace the next.

Decrease in office footprints
Some companies may reduce their overall office space due to the financial advantages of remote work. Instead of large centralized headquarters, there might be smaller satellite offices or hubs closer to where employees live.

A more globalized workforce and decentralization of work
More companies might look beyond traditional talent hubs and tap into talent from different regions or countries, leading to an even more globalized workforce. This could reduce demand for office spaces in traditionally expensive cities and increase demand in smaller towns or different countries.

Reallocation of resources away from real estate to other enablers
With potential reductions in required office space, companies might redirect their budgets. Savings from real estate might be invested in technology, employee training, or other growth areas.

The future of office design

The future of office design must incorporate both classical architecture and choice architecture, to ensure buildings and spaces within buildings are as relevant as possible. When employees are in the space, they need to be effective. The space needs to be agile and flexible enough to allow for evolving work projects. Some of the trends we might expect to see as a result include:

Increasingly tech-integrated spaces

As technology continues to evolve, offices will become increasingly integrated with advanced tech solutions. This includes IoT devices for optimizing energy use, advanced teleconferencing setups for virtual collaborations, and AI-driven solutions for security and efficiency.

More community and collaboration zones

While routine tasks might be performed remotely, offices will still serve as crucial hubs for team building, collaboration, and company culture. Expect more communal spaces designed for interaction and brainstorming.

Sustainable and eco-friendly designs

With growing awareness of environmental issues, future office designs will prioritize sustainability. This means more energy-efficient systems, sustainable building materials, and carbon-conscious designs.

Increased demand for coworking spaces

Freelancers, startups, and even larger corporations looking for flexibility will continue to turn to coworking spaces, leading to a boom in demand for these shared environments.

Enhanced connectivity infrastructure

As remote work becomes more common, there will be a push for improved digital infrastructure in both homes and offices. This means faster internet speeds, reliable connectivity, and dedicated spaces or tech for virtual meetings.

The future of employees

Employers need to think about employees as consumers. The retail industry tackled this challenge over fifteen years ago and continues to learn, adapt, and evolve. Companies need to understand that, in the conceptual age, the biggest assets breathe air, walk and talk, and vote with their feet. Expect to see more of the following:

Greater emphasis on wellbeing

The importance of employee wellbeing has come to the fore-front. Future office spaces will likely incorporate more natural light, green spaces, wellness centers, and ergonomic designs to boost employees' mental and physical health.

More focus on safety and health features

In the wake of the pandemic, offices might incorporate more health-focused features, such as better ventilation systems, touchless amenities, and spaces that can easily be modified for social distancing during health crises.

While these predictions are based on current trends and knowledge, and actual developments will vary based on unforeseen factors and innovations, they offer a glimpse into what we might expect to see as the future of work and office real estate.

And now for some loftier predictions...

Far-reaching predictions

Amara's law, coined by futurist Roy Amara, states that we tend to overestimate the effect of a technology in the short run and underestimate the effect in the long run. I expect the same to hold true in real estate. In that spirit, it's worth exploring some potentially more impactful predictions for the future that may take a bit longer to transpire.

Breaking the inertia of commercial real estate

Real estate, particularly commercial real estate, has been riding the wave of a seven trillion dollar asset class (retail and office space) for decades. The best example of the old way of doing things is the ribbon-cutting ceremony. Once the space or building was opened, it was considered "mission accomplished." In the conceptual age, office space will need to be as agile and flexible as hotel space. Here are some directions it may take:

The end of CRE

Corporate real estate as a defined practice is either dead or dying. Focusing merely on real estate or "place" is not enough. Tom Stat coined the phrase "splace," meaning immersive experiences. Space, place, and platforms.

Workplace experience is the combination of physical place, a coterie of employees, technology enabling those employees, and leadership to direct desired outcomes for the enterprise.

In the conceptual age, we must ask ourselves more meaningful questions beyond "Where?", "When?", "What?", and even "How?" work is addressed to focus on "Why?" and "Who?"

The end of traditional offices

Companies could abandon a majority of physical office spaces entirely in favor of digital workspaces, augmented reality conferences, and virtual reality collaborative zones.

Full digital integration
With advancements in AR and VR, remote employees might work in entirely simulated office environments, complete with virtual desks, meeting rooms, and even coffee breaks, offering a different kind of hybrid experience.

Dissolution of commercial real estate
Large commercial properties, such as office towers, might be repurposed into multiuse spaces, including residential units, urban farms, recreational centers, or community hubs.

AI and automation takeover
A majority of repetitive tasks, and even some high-level decision-making roles, might be taken over by AI, drastically reducing the human workforce in certain sectors.

Experience focused
Following the adaptation of retail, office will need to follow suit with a curated focus on experiences. The experience of third places will offer diversity in place, and encourage creativity and innovation. Expected trends in this area include:

Dynamic real estate
Buildings could become entirely modular and adaptable, changing their function based on real-time needs. A conference space in the morning could transform into a dining hall by evening and a recreational zone by night.

Renting personal workspaces
Instead of renting apartments or homes, individuals might rent personalized workspace modules in community hubs, while personal life becomes more nomadic or experience focused.

Experience economy boom

As basic work needs decrease due to automation, there might be a surge in industries focused on human experiences, wellness, entertainment, and personal growth. Real estate will pivot aggressively to cater to these sectors.

Healthy ecosystems

Healthy ecosystems involve live, work and play. This is a key area of focus for private and public leaders alike. Failure to form these healthy ecosystems leads to monocultures, which are doomed to fail. Here are some ideas:

Hyper-local living

With less need to commute, urban sprawl might reverse. People could opt to live in hyper-local communities where homes, recreation, shopping, and coworking spaces are all within walking or biking distance.

Living and working in transit

With the rise of autonomous vehicles, individuals might work and live in moving vehicles, offering a nomadic lifestyle while staying connected through advanced digital infrastructure.

Skill-based microcities

Entire cities or communities could be built around specific industries or skill sets, optimized entirely for that particular profession's needs, fostering innovation at an unprecedented scale.

Existential

At the time of writing, we are on the frontend of an office correction. While headlines portended a retail apocalypse following the global economic crisis, the industry adapted. The headlines are now screaming "office apocalypse." While much of it is hyperbole, as was the case with retail, there will be a reckoning. Existential trends include:

Environmental migration

As certain regions become less habitable due to climate change, there could be large-scale migrations to more sustainable regions, creating new hubs of work and innovation.

The future of work and the future of commercial real estate are both tied to the power of consumers, or employees. As highlighted throughout this book, design and delivery need to be agile to allow for the adaptation and evolution of real estate.

How will you flip VUCA?

We have much to learn from the consumer primacy impacting the retail world. Real estate decisions adapted and evolved to support the growing omnichannel retail business, but not without a lot of trial and error. Fortunately, the office sector has an opportunity to learn from retail's growing pains. Failure to acknowledge consumer primacy will cause immense economic suffering. Harnessing all the evolving tools, from GenAI to behavioral science, will strengthen portfolios and provide a product that consumers want to support.

Choice architecture is just as important as physical architecture, yet often overlooked. Design in every capacity, from the furniture and fixtures to the sustainable build focused on employee health and safety, must be considered.

Leadership will inspire and propel employees, not management-driven mandates. Companies must harness talent and drive effective outcomes, not just volume of work.

Leaders make the future, not managers. So, how will you flip VUCA? How will you move from volatility, uncertainty, complexity, and ambiguity to vision, understanding, clarity, and agility? For the commercial real estate world, agility is most important. That is, the ability to move quickly and easily, which is antithetical to the traditional approaches to real estate.

Today is the slowest rate of change of the rest of our lives. The rate of change *of* the rate of change (the second derivative of a function) shows the world is accelerating. Both owners and occupiers of real estate can "catch up" by leveraging and deploying technology in service of the consumer. Remember, the consumer is king.

10 key points to remember

Whether you own, occupy, service, or advise on real estate, the future of working and shopping needs to be curated by leaders who understand that a profound shift is underway. The shift is being driven by the exponential increase in technology and the resulting changes in human behavior. In order to best engage in the Work Shop world, I leave you with the following ten points:

1 Further develop your understanding of social science and/or behavioral economics and deploy choice architecture.

2 Onsite is the new offsite—remember to curate experiences.

3 Ribbon cuttings are the beginning, not the end.

4 Focus on insights over data. Data is oil in the ground with potential energy and value. Insights have kinetic energy.

5 Don't survey—people don't tell themselves the truth. Observe human behavior instead.

6 Focus on effectiveness over productivity, unless you are running a factory.

7 Today is the slowest day of change for the rest of your life. Act accordingly.

8 GenAI is the biggest platform shift in human history. How are you embracing the change?

9 Bigger change is coming. What are you doing to future-proof your business, your buildings, and your communities?

10 Put the consumer at the center of everything you do.

Now, armed with all of this new knowledge, I encourage you to go out and make the world a better space.

ACKNOWLEDGMENTS

N JUNE 2023, I left my position as CEO of Americas at The Instant Group. I was fortunate to lead and scale The Instant Group in the Americas, servicing clients and opening offices in all manner of places, from Buenos Aires and Mexico City to Toronto and throughout the United States. After traveling most days in most weeks, I found myself suddenly home every day. I'd like to thank my wife, Shannon, for her support. I asked her what she thought of me being home every day and the response remains the same... "It's weird." I'm still not sure if that's "good" weird or "bad" weird—but we are having fun and enjoying life. I love you, Shannon.

To our children, Grace and Joey. I'm beyond proud of the young adults you are becoming. Effort equals outcome and you both are proving it. I can't wait to see how you put your own dent in the universe.

I always cringed when someone called me "boss." I love being a leader but find the adage of boss to be somewhat out-dated. I always treat people with respect. You never know when you are going to work for them! To that end, I want to acknowledge some key people who influenced my working life and hopefully I've impacted theirs as well.

Thank you to Nestor Eliadis, Emily Watkins, Walter Wahlfeldt, Geno Coradini, Naveen Jaggi, Patrick Smith, Chris Noble, Rob Franks, Lew Kornberg, Steve Cutter, Josh Amoroso, Steve Panko, Ed Filer, Sam Maule, Luis Perez, Ben Wright, Michelle Bodick, Steve Rothman, Allie Lopez, Vincent Martino, Doug Sharp, Simon Foster, and most importantly, Durward W. Owen.

To the team at Grammar Factory, thanks for helping a first-time author and for making for process seamless and painless. You are all fantastic. Thanks to Scott MacMillan, Ania Ziemirska and Michelle Stevenson.

Many thanks to Andrea Kates for her ongoing guidance and advice. She is the Esther Perel of innovation and is busy helping people and organizations get "unstuck."

To Tom Stat, Yoda extraordinaire. Thanks for your friendship, guidance, and inspiration. I never knew things like VUCA, 42, and William Gibson quotes before engaging with you.

Finally, to my family. My sister Lisa Ann and brother-in-law Bob Miller, and sister Pam. Thanks for being siblings and friends. We need more cycling time in other parts of the world. And to my parents, Joe and Mary Ann Brady. Thanks for believing in me and allowing me to follow my path.

ABOUT
THE AUTHOR

JOE BRADY is a US-based commercial real estate expert with extensive experience in retail and office real estate. Having served in a number of senior roles at major companies, Brady has been at the forefront of accelerating technology, changing consumer behavior, and the evolution of real estate.

Brady previously served as CEO of Americas at The Instant Group, the global leader in agile and flexible workspace, development, and consulting. He led the company's growth through the COVID-19 pandemic in both North and South America, with offices across the US, Canada, Mexico, and Argentina. Under Brady's leadership, Instant grew fourfold.

Prior to The Instant Group, Brady was the head of real estate for Walgreens, managing a vast, 150 million square foot portfolio with an annual operating budget exceeding four billion dollars and an annual capital expenditure budget of one billion dollars. This role gave him in-depth experience in managing high-volume retail environments and implementing strategies for efficiency and growth.

Earlier in his career, Brady held senior positions at Jones Lang LaSalle (JLL), one of the world's leading professional services firms specializing in real estate and investment management. He was also a founder and partner of The Standard Group, acquired by JLL in 2008.

Brady is a global trustee of the International Council of Shopping Centers (ICSC), a member of Urban Land Institute (ULI) and CoreNet Global, a guest lecturer at the University of Florida's Warrington School of Business, a speaker, and an author. He holds a Bachelor of Electrical Engineering from Villanova University and an MBA from the University of North Carolina at Chapel Hill.

In 2024, Joe joined LRG Investors to grow the LRG brand nationally. Joe is married with two adult children and lives in Ponte Vedra Beach, Florida. His interests include almost anything outside, including flyfishing, skiing, golfing, and cycling.